A PROGRAMMED
INTRODUCTION
TO RESEARCH
Expanded Second Edition

SAMUEL LEVINE
FREEMAN F. ELZEY
San Francisco State University

Wadsworth Publishing Company, Inc.
Belmont, California

Designer: Paula Tuerk

Education Editor: Roger Peterson

Production Editor: Mary Arbogast　·

ISBN 0-534-00444-X

L. C. Cat. Card No. 76-2142

Printed in the United States of America

1 2 3 4 5 6 7 8 9 10---80 79 78 77 76

PREFACE

This programmed text provides instruction in what the
authors judge to be the essential concepts of experimental and nonexperimental hypothesis-testing research. It is designed for use in research methodology courses taught in the behavioral sciences during
the senior college year or first year of graduate
study.

It has been the writers' observation that students
taking research courses in the behavioral sciences
have greatest difficulty in understanding hypothesis-
testing research. Frequently, instructors in research methodology are unable to provide an adequate
orientation to hypothesis-testing research because
of the extensive coverage that must be offered within a single course.

This text presents the logic, technical terminology,
concepts, and some techniques used in research in
the behavioral sciences. No prior instruction in research methodology, statistics, or measurement is
assumed.

This enlarged edition of the text contains new programmed sets on the major threats to internal and external validity of research studies. Also, there
are programmed sets dealing extensively with preexperimental, experimental, and quasi-experimental
research designs. Each design is examined in terms
of the extent to which it controls for the various
threats to validity.

The previous edition of this text was field-tested
in four sections of a graduate course in educational
research. The rate of student error in frame responses was under 10 percent. Based on these field
tests and on the substantive criticism of colleagues,
the text was revised.

The authors wish to express their gratitude to
William Asher of the University of Pittsburgh,
William Kvaraceus of Tufts University, Merle C.
Wittrock of the University of California at Los
Angeles, and Enoch Sawin of San Francisco State College for their thoughtful criticisms and suggestions
during the development of the first edition. We are
greatly indebted to our colleagues, George Hallowitz,
Harold Jonsson, and C. Earl Miller, Jr., at San Francisco State College, who pretested and used the program for instructional purposes in their courses in
research methodology. Frederick J. McDonald and
John P. DeCecco were a continual source of encourage-
ment throughout the development of the program.

The expanded edition was reviewed in detail by
Thomas F. Butler of Pace University and Virgil
Walker of Bowie State College. Their comments and
criticisms were deeply appreciated.

CONTENTS

CORRELATION CHART FOR PROGRAMMED INTRODUCTION TO RESEARCH

		I	II	III	IV	V	VI	VII	VIII	IX
PART I	Introduction to Scientific Methodology (Sets 1, 2, & 3)	1	3	1	1, 3	1	1	1, 2	1	1, 2
PART II	Variables and Hypotheses (Sets 4, 5, & 6)	2, 4	2, 16	2	2, 3	1, 3	5	3	1, 2, 3	6, App.B
PART III	Sampling Techniques (Sets 7 & 8)	5	11	5	8	3	6	14	8	10
PART IV	Control of Extraneous Variables (Sets 9, 10, & 11)	4	16	8	17	8	12	13, 14	3, 5	9
PART V	Internal and External Validity (Sets 12 & 13)	4		8	18	8	12	14	5	9
PART VI	Research Designs (Sets 14, 15, & 16)	15	16	8	17, 18 19, 20	8	12	14	6	9
PART VII	Models for Structuring Research (Sets 17, 18, & 19)	15	16	8	17, 19 20	8	12	14	6	9
PART VIII	Use of Statistics in Research (Sets 20, 21, & 22)	11, 12	8		11, 12	App.B	12	14, 15	9	App.A

Roman numerals I through IX at the top of the chart indicate texts listed below the table. Numbers within the table are chapters of those texts.

AUTHORS FOR CORRELATION CHART:

I   Borg, W. R., & M. D. Gall. *Educational Research.* (2nd Ed.) New York: David McKay Co., 1971.

II Fox, D. J. *The Research Process in Education.* New York: Holt, Rinehart and Winston, 1969.

III Good, C. V. *Essentials of Educational Research.* New York: Appleton-Century-Crofts, 1966.

IV Kerlinger, F. N. *Foundations of Behavioral Research.* (2nd Ed.) Holt, Rinehart and Winston, 1973.

V   Rummel, J. F. *An Introduction to Research Procedures in Education.* (2nd Ed.) New York: Harper & Row, Publishers, 1964.

VI Sax, G. *Empirical Foundations of Educational Research.* Englewood Cliffs, N. J.: Prentice-Hall, 1968.

VII Travers, R. M. W. *An Introduction to Educational Research.* (2nd Ed.) New York: The Macmillan Company, 1964.

VIII Tuckman, B. W. *Conducting Educational Research: An Introduction.* (3rd Ed.) New York: McGraw-Hill Book Co., 1973.

INTRODUCTION

General texts in research cover a variety of topics and methodologies. Consequently, they are limited in the degree to which they provide instruction in hypothesis-testing research. This programmed text focuses explicitly on experimental and nonexperimental hypothesis-testing research.

Why this text is in programmed form. This text presents a new method for learning research methodology in which you (1) actively participate in every portion of the instructional process; (2) are presented with step-by-step instruction organized so that each step leads logically to the next; and (3) are allowed to proceed at your own pace through the program, moving quickly through those areas that present no difficulty and more slowly where you feel it necessary. After each finite step in the program, you are immediately informed of the correctness of your understanding. This immediate feedback is one of the important features of programmed instruction. It provides correction when necessary but, more important, it verifies when you have correctly grasped what is being taught.

How to use this programmed text. This program contains 22 sets grouped into eight parts. Before each part of the program a brief introductory statement describes the content of the programmed portion of the sets. You should read the

1:

introduction to each part carefully since it gives you a frame of reference for the instruction that follows.

Each set of the program contains a number of small units, called frames. Each frame presents some information and includes a blank space that you are to fill in. The correct response to each frame, which is given immediately below it, should be kept covered with a card or sheet of paper until after you have written your response to the frame.

You are given some cues as to the type of response required in each frame. For instance, the number and size of the blanks indicate the number and size of words required. In some frames, there are several alternatives from which to choose. For example, "Grass is_____(green/red/blue)." Some frames require you to provide a symbol. This is indicated by the word (symbol) following the blank. For example, "When you wish to express dollars you use___(symbol)."

A word of caution. For this programmed text to be most effective, you must follow the above instructions explicitly. Any shortcut reduces your chance of learning and retaining the research concepts and procedures covered. You should read each frame carefully, writing in your response to each blank provided in the frame. Keep the correct response below the frame *covered* until you have written in your response.

After responding, compare your response with the correct response below the frame. If your response is correct, proceed to the next frame. If your answer is incorrect, you should review the preceding frames in order to find out why you were incorrect. Make the necessary correction in your response before proceeding.

PART

I.

INTRODUCTION TO SCIENTIFIC METHODOLOGY

Frequently, actions are based on assumptions, be-
liefs, and untested generalizations. Such generalizations are usually accepted on faith or
authority and no attempt is made to verify their
correctness. But individuals are frequently faced
with problems for which they may have no ready-made
generalizations and limited or no previous experiences. In these instances, they may resort to
trial-and-error behavior. Such behavior is directed
toward arriving at some means of resolving problems
other than intentionally testing alternatives. As
a result, people may persist with limited, inappro-
priate, or ineffectual ways of behaving.

In contrast, research is concerned with the objective verification of generalizations. Such verification requires, on the one hand, the logical anal-
yses of problems and, on the other hand, the
devising of appropriate methodologies for obtaining
evidence.

Set 1 makes the distinction between testable and
nontestable general statements. Set 1 discusses
objective verification—as differentiated from
trial-and-error behavior or the acceptance of authority or faith. The importance of adequate definition to objective verification is mentioned.
Also, the purpose of research is to establish regularities between events or behaviors, which provide

generalizations useful for prediction and explanation. This set aids in understanding the difference between prediction and explanation. The concept of multiple rather than single causation is
stressed, and predictive statements are emphasized
in terms of antecedent and consequent factors
rather than in terms of cause and effect.

Set 2 introduces the inductive and deductive processes as they relate to objective verification.
The limitations of specific facts, events, or behaviors, and the importance of generalizations are
emphasized.

The requirements of conceptualizing behavior in
categorical terms and of determining those aspects
of behavior that are relevant to the phenomenon
being studied are introduced in Set 3. The relationship between facts and concepts is discussed
and differentiation is made between indicators and
instances of concepts.

1.

SCIENTIFIC VERIFICATION, PREDICTION, AND EXPLANATION

1 The methods used in research are usually referred
   to as scientific, to distinguish them from faith or
   belief. Religious dogma, because it is accepted on
   faith, is _____(scientific/nonscientific).

■ nonscientific

2 Similarly, "common sense" _____(would/would
   not) be considered scientific.

■ would not

3 Faith and authority are prescriptive and, therefore,
   _____(do/do not) encourage experimentation.

■ do not

4 The essential difference between faith and scientific inquiry is that the former accepts authority and
tradition whereas the latter proceeds from evidence
arrived at objectively. For example, the existence
of heaven and hell is accepted by some people on
faith and not because they have been verified
_____ .

■ objectively

5 Regardless of the usefulness of the concepts "heaven"
and "hell," they are not objectively verifiable and
therefore must be accepted on _____ .

■ faith

6 Verifying all statements of authority is not only
impossible but not necessarily desirable. For example, we generally accept a medical diagnosis on
faith rather than devising experiments to _____
the diagnosis objectively.

■ verify

7 We have faith in the physician's competence and act
according to his instructions. However, it should
be understood that the accuracy of the physician's
judgment could be objectively _____ if we
wished to do so.

■ verified

8 Frequently, actions are based on "hunches" or intuition. Such behavior depends on the appearance of
   what looks like the right approach. More likely
   than not, intuitive approaches lead to trial-and-
   _____ behavior.

■ error
■

9 It may take many trials and many errors before the
   occurrence of what appears to be a satisfactory out-
   come. Therefore, trial and error behavior is
   _____(efficient/inefficient).

■ inefficient
■

10 Of course, it is not always possible to know the
    best alternative before acting. However, there are
    logical and experimental bases for limiting the
    range of _____ before acting.

■ alternatives
■

11 Specifying meaningful alternatives is only one
    aspect of the scientific process. We must also be
    able to devise methodologies that permit us to
    _____ objectively which alternative is most ef-
    fective.

■ verify
■

12 Although trial and error is inefficient, it may be
    a more useful basis for behaving than acting on
    authority or _____ .

■ faith
■

13 Trial-and-error behavior may prove helpful in deter-
    mining meaningful alternatives which can then be
    tested _____ .

■
■   objectively

14 To carry the distinction between belief and objec-
    tive verification one step further, consider the
    belief that religious training leads to the "good
    life." It probably would not be difficult to
    determine the degree of formal religious training,
    but unless we can define the "good life" in terms
    that are _____ _____ we could not get
    scientific evidence regarding this belief.

■
■   objectively verifiable

15 Of course, we may not wish to test this belief; we
    may wish to act as though it were true. We would,
    then, accept the presumed relationship between re-
    ligious training and the "good life" on _____ .

■
■   faith

16 If we desired to test this belief we would first
    ask: what would suffice as evidence that an in-
    dividual was leading the "_____ _____"?

■
■   good life

17 In effect we would be seeking objective evidence of
something that we are willing to accept as the
"good life." For example, someone might suggest
that the "good life" is a moral life. We are still
faced with the necessity of defining a "moral life"
in such a way that it could be _____
_____ .

■ objectively verified

18 Assume that we are willing to accept as the definition of "moral life" lack of conflict with the law.
It should be evident that "conflict with the law"
_____(is/is not) more readily accessible to ob-
jective verification than is "moral life."

■ is

19 An experiment could be designed to test this supposition. If this supposition is valid, individuals
with high degrees of religious training generally
would show _____(less/greater) conflict with the
law than individuals with little or no religious
training.

■ less

20 The supposition regarding the virtue of religious
training was testable because we obtained _____
evidence of the "good" or "moral" life.

■ objective

21 Thus, to test the correctness of suppositions, it is necessary to obtain objective _____ .

■ evidence

22 In the natural sciences, such as chemistry or physics, there are relationships that have held true in every known instance. For example, the prediction that "objects of differing weights will fall at the same rate to speed in a vacuum" will _____ (sometimes/always) hold true.

■ always

23 Because lawful statements are invariant, the probability of their being supported is _____ (unity/less than unity).

■ unity

24 Predictions that hold true in every instance are lawful statements, which are _____ (variant/invariant).

■ invariant

25 The prediction in frame 22 about falling bodies in a vacuum _____ (is/is not) an example of a lawful statement.

■ is

26 In contrast to the physical sciences, the behavior-
    al sciences, such as education, psychology, and
    sociology, are concerned with predictions, which
    _____(are/are not) invariant.

■ are not

27 The statement "money leads to happiness"_____
    (is/is not) an invariant statement.

■ is not

28 Thus, in the behavioral sciences, although predic-
    tions may be lawful they are not _____ .

■ invariant

29 Predictions in the behavioral sciences are based on
    facts that _____(always/generally) hold true.

■ generally

30 Predictions are said to be *supported* by facts rather
    than proved by them, because behavioral scientists
    deal with probabilities that are _____ _____(less
    than/equal to) unity.

■ less than

31 The term "probabilistic statement" is confined to
    predictions whose probability is less than _____ .

■ unity/one

32 Research offers methodologies for obtaining facts to determine the probability of a _____ being supported.

■ prediction

33 General statements are usually arrived at from the observation of _____(few/many) instances.

■ many

34 Predictions about an individual _____(are/are not) as accurate as predictions about groups of people.

■ are not

35 If a person started a statement with "I once met one and he . . . ," we would suspect that general statements in regard to the group to which the "he" belonged would have a _____(low/high) probability of being supported.

■ low

36 Prediction from the observation of one instance is likely to lead to statements whose probability of support is _____(low/high).

■ low

37 probabilistic statements, then, are statements that
    may not be true for a specific individual but,
    rather, are generally true for a _____ .

■ group

38 Consider the following prediction: "children with
    IQs above 100 will read better than children with
    IQs below 100." The implication in this statement
    will be _____(always/generally) supported.

■ generally

39 It is possible that a child with a 94 IQ may read
    at a higher grade level than a child with a 102 IQ.
    This would indicate that the relationship between
    reading and IQ is less than _____ .

■ unity

40 The greater the probability of obtaining facts that
    support some general statement, the more accurate
    will be one's _____ .

■ predictions

41 The statement "most children will learn to read by
    age eight" is a(n) _____(prediction/explana-
    tion), but is not a(n) _____(prediction/
    explanation).

■ prediction, explanation

42 Seeking the "cause" for the occurrence of reading
    by age eight is seeking a(n) _____ .

■
■ explanation

43 The statement "he just happened to learn to read"
    _____(is/is not) an adequate explanation.

■
■ is not

44 An uncorrected visual defect _____(is/is not) a
    plausible explanation for not having learned to
    read.

■
■ is

45 The knowledge that behaviors are correlated is use-
    ful. However, correlations merely specify relation-
    ships; they do not _____ behavior.

■
■ explain

46 Theories relating to "will power"_____(are/are
    not) considered scientific explanations.

■
■ are not

47 Intuition and hunches are _____(scientif-
    ic/nonscientific) explanations.

■
■ nonscientific

48 Explanations that are not objectively verifiable
   are considered _____ .

■
■ nonscientific

49 Seeking scientific explanations essentially involves objective _____ of a "cause" or
   "causes."

■
■ verification

50 However, the occurrence of two events temporally or
   in sequence does not imply that one _____ the
   other.

■
■ causes

51 If it can be shown that the occurrence of an event
   requires the earlier presence of some other event,
   then a "_____-and-effect" relationship can be
   presumed.

■
■ cause

52 In the behavioral sciences we generally speak of
   antecedent factors rather than causal factors. An
   explanation, then, is a statement that relates
   a(n) _____ factor with a consequent factor.

■
■ antecedent

15:

53 A factor must be present antecedent to the consequent event in order for it to be a _____ .

∎ cause

54 Most behaviors are a result of multiple causation.
Therefore, behavioral scientists are usually concerned with _____ causation.

∎ multiple

55 Behavioral scientists caution individuals interested
in research not to think in terms of a single
_____ factor.

∎ causal

56 For an individual to learn to read, it may be necessary for him or her to have developed intellectually
to a particular level. Therefore, intellect would
be seen as one _____ factor in learning to read.

∎ causal

57 Intellect, then, may be a necessary factor in learning to read but it is not sufficient. Therefore,
there _____(are/are not) additional causal factors
in learning to read.

∎ are

58 Reading, then, is partially dependent upon intellect. The antecedent factors of education and
motivation may also be necessary _____ factors.

■ causal

59 Because there is likely to be more than one antecedent in learning to read, it is presumed that
reading is a product of _____ causation.

■ multiple

60 Because learning to read is multiply caused, attempts to predict learning rates from a single
antecedent are likely to be _____(accurate/
inaccurate).

■ inaccurate

61 Seeking to establish antecedent-consequent relationships is an attempt at explanation. An additional purpose, then, of scientific methodology is
_____ .

■ explanation

2:

INDUCTIVE AND DEDUCTIVE PROCESSES

1 Generalizations depend, in part, on the adequacy of the observations made. Therefore, it is best to make as many _____ as possible.

■ observations

2 A single instance does not provide a stable basis from which to _____ .

■ generalize

3 A single event _____(can/cannot) be described. We _____(can/cannot) generalize from it.

■ can, cannot

4 It is assumed that the observations we make do not result from chance but "truly" represent the phenomenon about which we seek to _____ .

■
■ generalize

5 The unique nature of single occurrences make generalizations risky because the event may have been a chance occurrence. Generalizations, then, are based on observable regularities and do not result from _____ .

■
■ chance

6 A generalization implies that the events observed are representative of similar events that could have been _____ .

■
■ observed

7 The statement "children with IQs above 100 read better than children with IQs below 100" specifies a regularity between IQ scores and reading ability. Such a statement is a _____ .

■
■ generalization

8 A generalization that is arrived at from a number of observations is called an inductive inference. Inferences arrived at by induction presume that the events observed in the past will occur in the _____ .

■
■ future

9 Generalizations arrived at from observed events are called _____ inferences.

∎ inductive

10 Unless we wish to remain entirely at the level of describing the past and present, prediction is a necessity. Inductive inferences are generalizations that are useful for making _____.

∎ predictions

11 In the behavioral sciences, the accuracy of prediction based on inductive inference will be _____ _____(equal to/less than) unity.

∎ less than

12 The validity of inductive inferences based on one instance of behavior probably will be _____(low/high).

∎ low

13 In order to arrive at valid generalizations from the process of inductive inference, we need to make _____(many/few) observations.

∎ many

14 A sufficient number of observations are necessary before the scientist attempts to arrive at a _____ .

∎ generalization

15   Thus, one of the requirements for arriving at a gen-
      eralization by induction is that you make a suffi-
      cient number of _____ .

■   observations

16   Because we are never able to observe all events,
      generalizations are almost always made on a limited
      number of observations. Such observations must be
      _____ in number in order to arrive at a gen-
      eralization.

■   sufficient

17   A biased sample of observations is one that is not
      representative of the population of observable
      events. If valid generalizations are to be made, in
      addition to being sufficient, the sample of observa-
      tions must also be _____ .

■   representative

18   The concept of representativeness presumes no bias
      in the _____ of observations.

■   sampling

19   Assume that two individuals have independently made
      a number of observations and, further, that these
      two individuals have inductively arrived at differ-
      ent generalizations. In this case, perhaps one or
      both individuals did not make a _____ number
      of observations, or the observations may not have
      been _____ .

■   sufficient, representative

20 Thus, the two requirements for arriving at generalizations by induction are that you make a _____
number of observations and that the observations be
_____ .

■ sufficient, representative

21 The requirement that sufficient and representative
observations be made is predicated on the fact that
it _____(is/is not) possible to observe every
instance of some phenomenon.

■ is not

22 "All children with IQs below 80 that I have ever observed could not learn to read until they were eight
years old. Therefore, all children that I will (or
can) observe in the future whose IQs are below 80
will not be able to learn to read until they are
eight years old." This is an example of a(n)
_____ inference.

■ inductive

23 Although the relationship between IQ and age relative to reading is stated in absolute terms, it is
assumed that such a relationship is merely
_____ .

■ probabilistic

24 Scientific methodology generally starts from the observation of particular events and arrives at a generalization by the process of _____ .

■ induction

25 The making of an inductive inference is moving from the particular to the _____ .

■
■ general

26 Conversely, deductive reasoning is moving from the general to the _____ .

■
■ particular

27 "All birds can fly. That object is a bird; there-fore it can fly." This is an example of _____ reasoning.

■
■ deductive

28 Inferences arrived at logically from a generaliza-tion are called _____ (inductions/deductions).

■
■ deductions

29 "All mentally retarded children do poorly on analyt-ic tasks." Using this generalization, the predic-tion that a particular mentally retarded child will do poorly on analytic tasks is a(n) _____ in-ference.

■
■ deductive

23:

30 The conclusion reached by deduction must be logical-
    ly consistent with two premises. The major premises
    stated in frame 29 is that all mentally retarded
    children will do poorly on _____ _____ .

■ analytic tasks

31 The minor premise in frame 29 is that the individual
    being observed is an instance of the people desig-
    nated as _____ _____ .

■ mentally retarded

32 Having identified an instance of the class of events
    (persons, behaviors, etc.) contained in the major
    premise, we can logically infer something about a
    particular instance. Such statements are called
    _____ inferences.

■ deductive

33 If the premises are accepted as true, it would be il-
    logical to conclude that a mentally retarded individ-
    ual would do _____(well/poorly) on analytic tasks.

■ well

34 In deductive reasoning, if one accepts the major and
    minor premises as true, the conclusion implied by
    the premises must be accepted as _____ .

■ true

35 The test of a prediction based on a generalization
    is a(n) _____(inductive/deductive) process.

■
■ deductive

36 Research is designed to test the validity of pre-
    dictions deduced from _____ .

■
■ generalizations

37 In the behavioral sciences, one _____(can/cannot)
    demonstrate the absolute truth of generalizations.

■
■ cannot

38 Each experimental instance that supports a deduction
    increases the _____ of a generalization.

■
■ validity

39 The usefulness of generalizations depends, in part,
    on one's being able to _____(induce/deduce) infer-
    ences from them.

■
■ deduce

40 In order to establish the validity of a generaliza-
    tion, it is important that we deduce inferences, or
    predictions, which are capable of _____ verifi-
    cation.

■
■ objective

41 Scientific methodology involves the process of inference. These inferences may be either _____ or
_____ .

■ inductive, deductive

42 In arriving at a generalization from particulars,
the essential process is _____ .

■ inductive

43 Predicting particulars from a generalization, or
coming to a conclusion from general premises, is essentially a(n) _____ process.

■ deductive

3∎

CONCEPTS,[1] INDICATORS, AND INSTANCES

1 The sentence "Mary's IQ is 82" is a factual statement about the intelligence of a _____ individual.

∎ specific/particular

2 "John is eight years old" is also a _____ statement about a particular individual.

∎ factual

---

[1] To simplify the presentation, the term "concept"
is used to include objective events in the environment such as chairs, height, or age, as well as in-
directly measured psychological phenomena such as
intelligence, motivation, and attitude. The latter
are usually referred to as "constructs."

3   Statements such as the above merely assert that
there exist instances that can be assigned to categories. Such instances are commonly known as
_____ .

■
■ facts

4   Categories of behaviors that have common characteristics are known as concepts. For example, the fact
that we can specify Mary's IQ indicates that there
exists a _____ known as intelligence.

■
■ concept

5   Mary's IQ is a _____ , whereas "intelligence" is a
_____ .

■
■ fact, concept

6   "John's reading achievement score is 3.2" _____
(is/is not) a concept.

■
■ is not

7   John's reading score is not a concept but a specific
_____ .

■
■ fact

8   Reading is a category of behavior that relates to
some underlying ability to recognize printed or written symbols. Reading, therefore, is a _____ .

■
■ concept

9 Of course, concepts need not refer solely to behaviors but can refer to objects as well. For example,
   because the word "chair" represents a category of objects that have certain characteristics in common,
   it is a _____ .

▪ concept

10 We could point to many instances of chairs, all of
    which would have certain characteristics of "chair-
    ness." The characteristics of the concept "chair"
    would be _____ (more/less) specific than the concept
    "intelligence."

▪ more

11 Memory as an aspect of intelligence is _____(more/
    less) abstract than intelligence.

▪ less

12 Repeating numbers, as an aspect of memory, is at a
    lower level of _____ than memory.

▪ abstraction

13 Concepts _____(do/do not) differ in their level
    of abstraction.

▪ do

14 A concept is an abstraction because it deals with
   the abstract rather than the _____ .

■ particular/specific

15 Individual facts are not scientifically useful in
   and of themselves. Science seeks regularities.
   Therefore, science seeks to establish facts that are
   _____ (general/specific).

■ general

16 The fact that Mary's IQ is 82 is of _____
   (limited/considerable) scientific usefulness.

■ limited

17 However, the concept "intelligence," defined as the
   potentiality to learn new tasks, is of considerable
   usefulness in that this concept has been shown to be
   systematically related to other _____ of interest to science.

■ concepts

18 From the above definition of intelligence, it would
   be safe to predict that, in general, individuals
   with high intelligence would be _____(poorer/
   better) readers than individuals with low intelligence.

■ better

19 Likewise, it would be safe to predict that individuals with high intelligence would be _____(poorer/better) in arithmetic than individuals with low intelligence.

■ better
■

20 The concept "intelligence" enters into systematic relationships with behaviors of interest to behavioral scientists. Therefore, concepts like intelligence have a _____(low/high) degree of usefulness.

■ high
■

21 Because standardized intelligence tests exist, instances of varying levels of intelligence _____ would/would not) be difficult to obtain.

■ would not
■

22 On the other hand, the objective verification of instances of degrees of anxiety _____(would/would not) present a problem.

■ would
■

23 Thus, all behaviors and events _____(can/cannot) be assessed with equal objectivity.

■ cannot
■

24 Although "IQ score 108" is an instance of the concept intelligence, the score itself _____ (does/
does not) indicate the behaviors included in the
assessment of intelligence.

■ does not

25 An individual with an IQ of 108 is an _____
(instance/indicator) of a concept.

■ instance

26 The ability to memorize can be called one _____
(instance/indicator) of the behaviors included in
the assessment of intelligence.

■ indicator

27 Thus, instances and indicators _____ (are/are not)
synonymous.

■ are not

28 To determine an instance of a concept, we must first
specify _____ of the concept.

■ indicators

29 If we wish to assess intelligence we must determine
the _____ of intelligence.

■ indicators

30 If we include memory in a test of intelligence, then
we are accepting _____ as one indicator of intelligence.

■
■ memory

31 Most people would question the inclusion of solely
memory-type behaviors in a test of intelligence.
Therefore, additional _____ of intelligence
should be specified.

■
■ indicators

32 If, in addition to memory, we added the ability to
abstract as an indicator of intelligence, we would
increase the accuracy in categorizing _____ of
"high" and "low" IQs.

■
■ instances

33 We would expect that indicators of height would be
_____(more/less) specific than indicators of intel-
ligence.

■
■ more

34 Determining a person's height is likely to be more
accurate than determining his or her intelligence because the _____ of height can be assessed
with greater objectivity.

■
■ indicators

35 Accuracy in determining an instance is dependent
    upon how specific the indicators are which represent
    the _____ .

■
■ concept

36 Accurate categorization, then, requires the clear
    specification of the _____ of concepts.

■
■ indicators

37 Although "sweating of the hands" is defined by some
    as an indicator of anxiety, it is not highly agreed
    upon, mainly because "sweating" may be a(n)
    _____ of other things as well.

■
■ indicator

38 Although sweating of the hands is specific, the prob-
    lem arises as to what may be inferred from this phe-
    nomenon. If "sweating" is primarily determined by
    physiology, independent of anxiety, then "sweating"
    would be a _____(good/poor) indicator of anxiety.

■
■ poor

39 In contrast, memory is a highly agreed upon
    _____ of intelligence.

■
■ indicator

40 The indicators of anxiety would be _____(more/less) difficult to specify than those of intelligence.

■ more

41 Many of the indicators of intelligence are highly agreed upon, whereas the _____ of anxiety are not.

■ indicators

42 Thus, at this stage of behavioral research, it is likely that categorizing individuals as "highly" anxious is _____(more/less) accurate than categorizing individuals as "highly" intelligent.

■ less

43 In order to test the prediction "children who are breast fed show less anxiety than children who are bottle fed," we must specify indicators of anxiety as well as indicators of the methods of _____ .

■ feeding

44 It would be difficult to obtain support for the prediction if we cannot agree upon the _____ of anxiety.

■ indicators

45 Although "breast" and "bottle" can be differentiated as indicators, it _____(is/is not) likely that all children will have been completely fed on one or the other.

■ is not

46 Nevertheless, categorizing instances of children who are breast fed or bottle fed is necessary to support the prediction. A child who has never been fed by bottle or other artificial means is an obvious _____ of breast feeding.

■ instance

47 Categorizing a child who has been fed by both methods will present some difficulty. To test this prediction we could take a severe position on this and accept only pure _____ of one or the other.

■ instances

48 To specify indicators of concepts, the usual procedure is to provide a definition of the _____ .

■ concept

49 The concept "type of feeding" has two categories— "breast fed" and "bottle fed." We must define these categories of the general concept _____ (separately/inclusively).

■ separately

50 The categories should be defined separately so that
    the _____ of one category are not those of
    the other category.

■
■ indicators

51 That is, there should be no overlap in the _____
    that define the categories "breast fed" and "bottle
    fed."

■
■ indicators

52 If the indicators of the category "breast fed" were
    precisely identical with those of the category
    "bottle fed," there would be no way to distinguish
    between _____ of breast feeding and bottle
    feeding.

■
■ instances

53 "Use of an artificially constructed container with a
    nipple at one end" is likely to be an indicator of
    the category _____(breast/bottle) fed.

■
■ bottle

54 A child fed with such a device would be an instance
    of the _____ "bottle fed."

■
■ category

37:

55 The words in the definition in frame 53 that indicate "bottle feeding" rather than "breast feeding"
are: _____ _____ .

■ artificially constructed

56 Because the word "nipple" is common to both categories, by itself it is a _____ (good/poor) indicator
for selecting instances of bottle fed and breast fed
children.

■ poor

57 The indicator nipple in the definition of "bottle
fed" defines _____ of non-breast fed children.

■ instances

58 For example, the indicator "nipple" _____ (does/
does not) permit the inclusion in the study of children who have been fed primarily by intravenous
means.

■ does not

59 To further narrow the instances that may be categorized as bottle fed, we could specify that the
feeding must be through the child's mouth. Intake
through the mouth now becomes a(n) _____ .

■ indicator

60 However, although "intake through the mouth" makes
more specific the category "bottle fed," this indicator _____ (is/is not) helpful for distinguishing
between the two categories of the concept "type of
feeding."

■ is not

61 An infant fed intravenously is not fed by nipple or
by mouth and cannot be a(n) _____ of the category "bottle fed."

■ instance

62 Dropper feeding does not include the indicator
_____(nipple/mouth).

■ nipple

63 A child fed by a dropper _____(would/would not)
be an instance of the category "bottle fed."

■ would not

64 To test the prediction about anxiety and type of
feeding, it will be necessary to define each type of
feeding, besides defining anxiety. Vague indicators
will create difficulty in the selection of
_____ to be categorized as bottle fed or
breast fed.

■ instances

PART

VARIABLES AND HYPOTHESES

As pointed out in the introductory sets, not all generalizations or theories are testable. In research,
the validity of generalizations is determined by
testing deductions made from them.
   In Sets 4, 5, and 6 the relationship between antecedent and consequent events is further developed.
The concepts used in research are given particular
terms and relate to anticipated behavioral changes
as well as to manipulations designed to produce or
change behavior. Set 4 differentiates between dependent and independent variables and relates them
to the testing of logical consequences deduced from
generalizations. Set 5 teaches how to relate dependent and independent variables so as to state predictions in hypothetical terms. Directional and nondirectional hypotheses are differentiated. Criteria
for evaluating the adequacy of hypotheses are offered. Set 6 distinguishes between experimental and
nonexperimental research, differentiates between experimental and control groups, and underscores the
importance of maximizing treatment effects.

4.

DEPENDENT AND INDEPENDENT VARIABLES

1 Not all concepts are of scientific interest. There are many concepts that describe the world and events but are not useful for explanation or _____ .

■ prediction

2 The fact that we have concepts representing such things as bookshelves, chairs, doors, and cows does not require that we attempt to relate them to other _____ .

■ concepts

3 Of particular interest to behavioral scientists are concepts that enter into systematic relationships with other concepts, and are useful for _____ and _____ .

■ explanation, prediction

4 A concept that can take on different quantitative or
   qualitative values is called a variable. The concept of intelligence can take on various values from
   low to high. Therefore, intelligence can be termed
   a _____ .

■ variable

5 Variables are _____ that serve a particular purpose in research.

■ concepts

6 If we wish to study the relationship between height
   and nutrition, both height and nutrition would be
   considered as _____ .

■ variables

7 Phenomena that can take on quantitatively different
   values are called continuous variables. Chronological age is an example of a _____(continuous/
   noncontinuous) variable.

■ continuous

8 The fact that we can distinguish degrees of a variable indicates that the phenomenon underlying the
   variable _____(is/is not) continuous.

■ is

9 Socioeconomic status varies from low to high and is
an example of a _____ variable.

■ continuous

10 When variables are said to be continuous, the impli-
cation is that the phenomena underlying the indicators of the variables are likewise _____ .

■ continuous

11 Not all variables are continuous. The variable of
sex when categorized as male and female _____(is/
is not) an example of a continuous variable.

■ is not

12 Although the variable of sex when categorized as
male and female is treated as noncontinuous, the variable masculinity-feminity would be considered
_____ .

■ continuous

13 If we wished to compare the temperaments of women
with blond, brown, black, and red hair (in the natural state), color of hair would be considered a
_____(continuous/noncontinuous) variable.

■ noncontinuous

14 As discussed previously, some variables are antecedent to other variables. To be able to read, it is
presumed that an individual needs to have some degree of intelligence. Therefore, the variable
"intelligence" would be _____ to the variable
"reading."

■ antecedent
■

15 To speak of one variable being a consequence of another variable is to stipulate that the former is
_____ _____(dependent upon/independent of)
the latter.

■ dependent upon
■

16 In part, reading is a _____ of the variable
"intelligence."

■ consequence
■

17 Reading ability is _____ upon the individual's
intelligence level.

■ dependent
■

18 An individual's age _____(is/is not) dependent
upon the individual's height.

■ is not
■

19 Height, besides being dependent upon age, is also
_____ upon the individual's sex.

■ dependent

20 In research, the variables that are a consequence of
antecedent variables are called _____ variables.

■ dependent

21 Although height is dependent upon age, age _____
(is/is not) dependent upon height.

■ is not

22 Age, then, is _____ _____(dependent on/inde-
pendent of) height.

■ independent of

23 Variables that are antecedent to the dependent variable are called _____ variables.

■ independent

24 In testing the relationship between sex and speed in
running, speed is the _____ variable and sex
is the _____ variable.

■ dependent, independent

25 "Children who are breast fed are less anxious than children who are bottle fed." In this statement the dependent variable is _____ .

■ anxiety

26 Anxiety is considered as the dependent variable because it is a _____ of the type of feeding.

■ consequence

27 The type of feeding is the _____ variable because it is _____ to the variable "anxiety."

■ independent, antecedent

28 The dependent variable, anxiety, is continuous, whereas the independent variable, type of feeding, is _____ .

■ noncontinuous

29 Knowing whether a variable is continuous or noncontinuous will be of help later in the data analysis. Variables usually expressed quantitatively by scores of some kind are called _____ variables.

■ continuous

30 Variables that categorize individuals in nonquantitative terms are called _____ variables.

■ noncontinuous

31 "Students behind their grade level in achievement show a greater frequency of dropout than students who are above grade level in achievement." The dependent variable is _____ ____ _____ .

■ frequency of dropout

32 The independent variable is _____ .

■ achievement

33 The frequency of dropout is _____ upon achievement.

■ dependent

34 "Children grouped heterogeneously show greater gains in reading achievement than children homogeneously grouped." The dependent variable is _____ _____ .

■ reading achievement

35 The type of grouping is the _____ variable.

■ independent

36 In our previous examples, conditions manipulated by the researcher—such as type of feeding and type of grouping—are called _____ variables.

■ independent

37 Variables dealing with behavioral responses are called _____ variables.

■ dependent

38 Behavioral scientists are concerned with the influence of independent variables on the behavioral _____ of people.

■ responses

39 Behaviors that are influenced by environmental conditions or antecedent behaviors are called _____ variables.

■ dependent

40 In studies of students' reading abilities, the methods of teaching reading would be _____ variables.

■ independent

41 The mode of instruction, such as ready-made films and lectures, is an example of an _____ variable.

■ independent

42 The examples in frame 41 are called independent variables because they are manipulations of the environment that _____(are/are not) under the control of the researcher.

■
■ are

43 The decision to manipulate the environment in a particular way is made _____(antecedent/consequent) to observing behavioral changes in people.

■
■ antecedent

44 The behavioral changes that occur as a result of the environmental manipulations are called _____ variables.

■
■ dependent

45 Because the objectives of the school are to bring about specified behavior changes in children, such objectives may be termed _____ variables.

■
■ dependent

46 Teaching methodologies and procedures are instances of _____ variables.

■
■ independent

47 Before we can select the independent variables for manipulation, we must be clear as to the changes in people's _____ we wish to study.

■ behavior

48 Behavioral changes _____(are/are not) presumably dependent upon other behaviors as well as upon environmental _____ .

■ are, manipulations

49 The previous examples have included manipulated and nonmanipulated independent variables.[1] Type of reading instruction is an example of a _____ independent variable, whereas, sex is an example of a _____ independent variable.

■ manipulated, nonmanipulated

50 Environmental manipulations under the control of the researcher are _____ independent variables.

■ manipulated

---

[1] Some authors prefer to restrict the term "independent variable" solely to manipulated variables. However, in the behavioral sciences many research designs include both variables that are attributes of people and independent variables that are manipulations of the environment. In this text, where the distinction is necessary, attributes of people are referred to as nonmanipulated independent variables to differentiate them from manipulated independent variables.

51 Variables such as IQ, reading ability, and socioeco-
    nomic status are attributes of people and are
    _____ independent variables.

■ nonmanipulated

52 Behaviors may be both independent and dependent vari-
    ables. However, environmental conditions or manipu-
    lations are always _____ variables.

■ independent

53 Whether a behavior is a dependent or an independent
    variable will depend on the purpose of the study.
    If the effect of motivation on achievement is to be
    studied, then motivation is treated as the
    _____ variable.

■ independent

54 In the case of frame 53, the student's achievement
    is _____ upon motivation.

■ dependent

55 However, if we wish to determine the effect of
    grading procedures on motivation, then motivation is
    the _____ variable.

■ dependent

56 It would be illogical to think that the grading procedure is affected by students' motivation because
the grading procedure is initiated _____ to
the measure of the students' motivation.

■
■ antecedent

57 Intelligence, as a relatively stable characteristic
of an individual at a particular time, is not usually the explicit focus of a study of behavioral
change. Therefore, intelligence is usually treated
as a(n) _____ variable.

■
■ independent

58 However, some years back a series of studies was conducted in Iowa to determine the effects of different
types of living situations on the intelligence of
children. In this case, intelligence was the
_____ variable.

■
■ dependent

59 Chronological age cannot normally be affected by any
procedure except the passage of time, which is not
under the control of man (as yet). Therefore, chronological age is always treated as a(n) _____
variable.

■
■ independent

60 Assessing the effectiveness of the _____ var-
    iable in bringing about changes in the _____
    variable is the usual procedure for objectively veri-
    fying predictions.

■   independent, dependent

SET

5∎

HYPOTHESES

1 "Breast fed children will show less anxiety than
   bottle fed children." This statement is a
   _____(fact/prediction).

∎ prediction

2 The type of feeding—whether by breast or bottle—is
   the _____ variable.

∎ independent

3 Anxiety, as a presumed consequence of the type of
   feeding, is the _____ variable.

∎ dependent

4 The above prediction, then, contains two variables:
   a(n) _____ and a(n) _____ variable.

∎ independent, dependent

5 Predictions are hypothesized relationships. Therefore, predictions that are tested by scientific
methods are termed research _____ .

■ hypotheses

6 A researcher made this prediction: "Children who receive counseling will show a greater increase in cre-
ativity than children not receiving counseling."
This prediction is to be tested and, therefore, this
statement is the research _____ of the study.

■ hypothesis

7 This research hypothesis, like the previous one, contains a(n) _____ and a(n) _____ varia-
ble.

■ independent, dependent

8 A research hypothesis, then, is a predictive statement that relates a(n) _____ variable to a(n)
_____ variable.

■ independent, dependent

9 A statement that contains only one variable _____
(does/does not) meet the definition of a research
hypothesis.

■ does not

10 A statement that contains two dependent variables *but no independent* variable _____ (does/does not) meet the definition of a research hypothesis.

■ does not

11 A research hypothesis must contain at least one _____ and one _____ variable.

■ independent, dependent

12 Predictive statements that cannot be objectively verified _____ (should/should not) be called research hypotheses.

■ should not

13 Similarly, relationships that are assumed but are not meant to be tested _____ (are/are not) research hypotheses.

■ are not

14 "Children who receive immediate feedback show greater gains in arithmetic achievement than children who receive delayed feedback." This statement _____ (is/is not) a research hypothesis.

■ is

15 In frame 14 the condition that is varied is the _____ .

■ feedback

16 The type of feedback is the _____ variable.

■ independent

17 The dependent variable is _____ _____ .

■ arithmetic achievement

18 We may assume that, in part, the reason immediate feedback is more effective than delayed feedback is because it increases motivation. Motivation is not to be tested explicitly and it _____(is/is not) treated as an independent or dependent variable.

■ is not

19 However, we could seek to verify objectively the relationship between motivation and _____ .

■ feedback

20 If we were to hypothesize a relationship between motivation and feedback, motivation would be the _____(independent/dependent) variable.

■ dependent

21 Motivation is dependent upon the type of _____ .

■ feedback

22 The type of feedback is the _____ (independent/dependent) variable.

■ independent

23 It is likely that we would predict greater increases in motivation for the _____ (immediate/delayed) feedback group.

■ immediate

24 It may well be that the motivation of both groups will increase. However, the research hypothesis stipulates a differential increase in favor of the _____ feedback group.

■ immediate

25 The researcher can control the assignment of children to the immediate and delayed feedback groups. In other words, he is free to manipulate the _____ variable.

■ independent

26 The researcher cannot directly manipulate the _____ of the groups assigned to one or the other type of feedback.

■ motivation

27 Increases in motivation are presumably a consequence
of the type of feedback. Motivation, then, is
_____ upon the type of feedback.

■ dependent

28 There may be a number of factors in the learning sit-
uation that affect motivation. However, the variable that has been introduced and on which the two
groups are known to differ is _____ .

■ feedback

29 We assume that the two groups have similar learning
situations except for the introduction of the
_____ variable.

■ independent

30 If the assumption is correct, then differences in
the increase in motivation between the two groups
can be attributed to the _____ variable.

■ independent

31 If the immediate feedback group increases in motivation more than the delayed feedback group, there
is support for the research _____ .

■ hypothesis

32 To verify objectively a research hypothesis, it is necessary to define operationally both the _____ and _____ variables.

■ independent, dependent

33 It is necessary to specify the indicators of the variables to verify objectively the research _____ .

■ hypothesis

34 One criterion of the adequacy of a research hypothesis is whether it can be objectively _____ .

■ verified

35 If a research hypothesis is testable, it is said to be _____ .

■ verifiable

36 Proper definition is only one aspect of evaluating whether a hypothesis is testable. The specification of appropriate conditions and the availability of specified populations are additional factors necessary for a hypothesis to be _____ .

■ testable

37 "Children who do not achieve oedipal resolution be-
    fore age eight will show a greater degree of alcohol-
    ism as adults than will children who do." This hy-
    pothesis requires specification of the indicators of
    the variables of _____ _____ and

    _____ .

■ oedipal resolution, alcoholism

38 A major difficulty in testing this hypothesis is
    specifying the _____ of oedipal resolution.

■ indicators

39 Apart from the problem of definition, there is a con-
    siderable period of time between the occurrence of
    the _____ variable, oedipal resolution, and
    the consequence, alcoholism.

■ independent/antecedent

40 Because of the tremendous number of intervening ex-
    periences between oedipal resolution and the onset
    of alcoholism, this hypothesis is probably
    _____ (testable/nontestable).

■ nontestable

41 "A curriculum oriented toward inquiry training will
    increase children's thinking ability more than a
    didactic-oriented curriculum will." This statement
    is a research _____ .

■ hypothesis

42 The type of curriculum orientation is the
    _____ variable.

■ independent

43 Thinking ability is the dependent variable because
    it is a(n) _____ (antecedent/consequence) of
    the type of curriculum.

■ consequence

44 "Thinking ability" is an extremely general term
    making objective _____ impossible without
    further specification.

■ verification

45 "Thinking ability" could refer to the memory of spe-
    cific facts or to the development of theories. The
    behavioral indicators of these aspects of thinking
    would be quite _____(alike/different).

■ different

46 A further aspect of the testability of a hypothesis
    is the specificity of the _____ that enter in-
    to the hypothesis.

■ variables

47 "Mentally retarded children who attend public school
programs will show greater increases in social competence than will such children attending institutional school programs." This research hypothesis
states that the children attending the _____
school program will do better than those attending
the _____ school program.

■ public, institutional
■

48 The direction of the difference in changes between
the two groups _____(has/has not) been stipu-
lated.

■ has
■

49 A research hypothesis that stipulates the direction
a comparison will take is termed a _____
(directional/nondirectional) hypothesis.

■ directional
■

50 This study compares the effects of two types of
school programs and therefore is stated in terms of
the _____ in the increase on the dependent
variable.

■ difference
■

51 "There will be a positive relationship between an individual's attitudes toward racial minorities and
his socioeconomic status." This research hypothesis
stipulates that individuals with favorable attitudes
will generally come from _____(higher/lower)
socioeconomic groups.

■ higher
■

52 This hypothesis _____ (does/does not) stipulate the direction of the relationship.

■
■ does

53 The hypothesis is a _____ (directional/non-directional) one.

■
■ directional

54 A directional research hypothesis, then, may be stated in terms of expected relationships or expected _____ between groups.

■
■ differences

55 "There will be a difference in the adaptability of fathers and mothers toward the rearing of their children." Although this hypothesis stipulates there will be a difference, the _____ of the difference is not specified.

■
■ direction

56 Although the researcher may wish to determine the direction of the difference, the research hypothesis is stated in _____ terms.

■
■ nondirectional

57 Whereas the researcher in frame 47 predicted that a particular group would outperform another, the researcher in frame 55 _____(did/did not) do so.

■
■ did not

58 Thus, the researcher in frame 47 expects his results to show differences in _____(one/either) direction.

■
■ one

59 The researcher in frame 55 is interested in testing differences in _____(one/either) direction.

■
■ either

60 A research hypothesis that specifies the direction of expected differences or relationships is called a _____ research hypothesis.

■
■ directional

61 A research hypothesis that does not specify the direction of expected differences or relationships is called a _____ research hypothesis.

■
■ nondirectional

6∎

EXPERIMENTAL AND NONEXPERIMENTAL HYPOTHESIS-
TESTING RESEARCH

STUDY 6-1

A researcher tested the hypothesis that fifth
grade boys and girls differed in arithmetic
achievement. Using knowledge of the processes by
which boys and girls are socialized, the researcher predicted that boys would score higher
than girls. He randomly selected 50 students of
each sex and performed a statistical test of the
difference between their arithmetic achievement
test scores.

---

1 The independent variable in Study 6-1 is the _____
of the student.

∎ sex

2 In Study 6-1 the independent variable _____(was/
was not) manipulated.

∎ was not

3 No new condition was introduced nor was an aspect of the environment manipulated. This establishes Study 6-1 as _____ (experimental/nonexperimental).

▪ nonexperimental

4 Study 6-1 is nonexperimental and the hypothesis tested _____ (is/is not) directional.

▪ is

5 Study 6-1 is an example of directional hypothesis-testing research because the _____ of the difference between the males and females is specified.

▪ direction

6 Comparing the health problems of children from low, middle and high socioeconomic groups _____(is/is not) an example of nonexperimental hypothesis-testing research because the _____ variable is not _____ .

▪ is, independent, manipulated

7 Research in which an independent variable is not manipulated is termed _____ _____-_____ research.

▪ nonexperimental hypothesis-testing

```
STUDY 6-2

A researcher wished to determine the relative ef-
fectiveness of two methods of perceptual skill
training on third grade children's reading abil-
ity. He randomly selected two groups of chil-
dren and gave each group a different method for
the entire school year. The reading ability of
the two groups was measured, using a standard
reading test, at both the beginning and end of
the school year.
```

8 The independent variable in Study 6-2 is the
_____ _____ _____ and the dependent
variable is _____ _____ .

■ perceptual skill training, reading ability

9 In Study 6-2 the researcher introduced two methods
of perceptual skill training. By so doing the independent variable _____(was/was not) manipulated.

■ was

10 Study 6-2 is an example of a second type of
hypothesis-testing research. This is research in
which the _____ variable is intentionally
manipulated.

■ independent

```
STUDY 6-3

The Center for Developmental Studies assessed
changes in children's cognitive development as
they progressed from age two through eight.  On
the children's birthdates they were given a bat-
tery of cognitive tests.  As a side study, some
of the children in one age group were given spe-
cial cognitive games for a period of one year
and compared with the remainder of the children
of their age not receiving such games.
```

11 Study 6-3 is a longitudinal developmental study describing children's increase in cognitive development, the _____ variable.

■
■ dependent

12 In Study 6-3 the independent variable is the _____
of the children.

■
■ age

13 Age, as the independent variable, changes "naturally"
and therefore is not _____ by the researcher.

■
■ manipulated

14 Thus, this study is an example of _____
(experimental/nonexperimental) hypothesis-testing
research.

■
■ nonexperimental

15 Study 6-3 is primarily nonexperimental, but the introduction of cognitive games for comparative purposes provides an element of _____ research.

■ experimental

16 The experimental study within a nonexperimental longitudinal study is not the usual case. More frequently, longitudinal studies remain at a descrip-
   tive level and do not involve the _____ of
   an independent variable.

■ manipulation

17 If a survey of opinions on educational issues was
   conducted for a number of successive years, the survey normally _____(would/would not) involve
   the manipulation of an independent variable.

■ would not

18 Thus, surveys conducted at periodic intervals are of
   the _____(experimental/nonexperimental)
   type.

■ nonexperimental

19 The primary difference between experimental and nonexperimental hypothesis-testing research is that in
   the former the independent variable _____(is/
   is not) manipulated, whereas in the latter the independent variable _____(is/is not) manipulated.

■ is, is not

20 In hypothesis-testing research it is necessary to have a comparative basis for evaluating group differences. Therefore, hypothesis-testing research requires _____(one/two or more) groups.

■ two or more

STUDY 6-4

From a group of students who were to take social studies, the researcher randomly selected 50 students. He then divided them into two groups by randomly assigning 25 to Group X, the usual social studies program, and 25 to Group Y, a novel program designed to deal with the history of particular ethnic groups. At the end of the school semester he administered a test of "Ethnic Understanding" to each group.

---

21 Study 6-4 is a(n) _____(experimental/non-experimental) study.

■ experimental

22 The independent variable in Study 6-4 is _____ _____(type of social studies program/ethnic understanding).

■ type of social studies program

23 By the designations used to describe the independent variable in Study 6-4, the _____ social studies program is of a nontraditional nature.

■ novel

24 Group ___(X/Y) is to receive the novel program whereas Group ___ (X/Y) will receive the usual social
studies program.

■ Y, X

25 A group that is exposed to usual conditions is termed a control group. In Study 6-4, the control group
is Group ___(X/Y).

■ X

26 Group X is termed the control group in Study 6-4 because it was exposed to _____(usual/novel) conditions.

■ usual

27 A group exposed to some novel condition is termed an
experimental group. In Study 6-4 the experimental
group is Group ___(X/Y).

■ Y

28 Group Y is an experimental group because it was exposed to _____(usual/novel) conditions.

■ novel

29 If both groups X and Y had been exposed to novel social studies programs, both groups would be termed
_____ groups.

■ experimental

30 Thus, it is possible to design studies that include only experimental groups, or studies that include both experimental and _____ groups.

■ control

31 Comparing groups under differing conditions affords a basis for determining the relative effectiveness of the _____(independent/dependent) variable.

■ independent

32 Study 6-4 is an example of _____(directional/nondirectional) hypothesis-testing research.

■ directional

33 In effect, the directional hypothesis in Study 6-4 stipulates that the _____ social studies program will prove more powerful than the _____ program in producing changes in the dependent variable.

■ novel, usual

34 In Study 6-4 "usual" and "novel" were used to differentiate the control from the _____ group.

■ experimental

35 The greater the differences in the operations of the
    programs the _____ (less/more) likely it is they
    will defferentially affect the dependent variable.

■
■   more

36 The terms "usual" and "novel" do not convey the pre-
    cise nature of the social studies programs being com-
    pared. However, we would expect that the two pro-
    grams would differ _____ (minimally/maximally).

■
■   maximally

37 In directional hypothesis-testing research, one con-
    dition of the independent variable (such as "novel"
    condition) is presumed to influence the _____
    _____ systematically differently from the other
    condition of the independent variable.

■
■   dependent variable

38 Directional hypotheses do not require a manipulated
    independent variable for the prediction of group dif-
    ferences. Predictions of group differences on the
    dependent variable may be based on categories of a
    _____ independent variable.

■
■   nonmanipulated

39 As with manipulated independent variables, the
    greater the difference between categories of nonma-
    nipulated independent variables the greater the like-
    lihood that there will be a differential effect on
    the _____ variable.

■
■   dependent

40 For example, assume a researcher wished to determine the effects of socioeconomic status on reading ability. Comparing "low" socioeconomic status students with "high" socioeconomic status students is likely to lead to _____(smaller/larger) group differences in reading ability than comparing "high" and "middle" socioeconomic status students.

∎ larger

41 In sum, whether the independent variable is manipulated or not or whether the hypothesis is directional or nondirectional, the differences between conditions or categories of the _____ _____ should be maximal.

∎ independent variable

III.

SAMPLING TECHNIQUES

In the behavioral sciences, one purpose of research is to provide methods and techniques that permit inference from a selected sample to the population from which the sample was drawn. For these inferences to be valid, the selection of the sample must be made in such a manner that it is representative of the population.

Sets 7 and 8 introduce the concepts and techniques relevant to sampling. The purpose of sampling is discussed and the definitions of population and sample, as used in research, are given. The concepts of representativeness in sampling and sampling bias are introduced, and their effect upon generalizing research findings is discussed. The techniques of "simple random" and "stratified" sampling are presented and examples of each are given. A number of exercises—including the use of a table of random numbers—provide practice in applying these techniques.

SET

7 ⏸

POPULATION, SAMPLE, AND RANDOM SAMPLING

1 If we assess the reading achievement of all third graders in a city, we have measured the total population of such children in that city. If we obtain the running speed in the 100 meter dash for *all* competitors in the Olympics, we have data on the total _____ of this description.

■ population

2 A population is determined by its defining characteristics. Thus, if our defining characteristics are eighth grade boys in the midwest, the population includes _____(all/some) children who have these characteristics.

■ all

3 For such a population, the defining characteristics are that they are boys in the _____ grade, and they reside in the _____ .

■ eighth, midwest

4   When we obtain measures of all individuals who have
    these defining characteristics, we have measured the
    _____ .

■   population
■

5   If the defining characteristics of a population are
    children who are in the third grade in a city, a
    girl who is in the fifth grade _____(would/
    would not) be an element of the population.

■   would not
■

6   If we assess the reading achievement of all the
    third graders in a city we have measured the total
    population having these defining _____ .

■   characteristics
■

7   It is likely there are many third graders in San
    Francisco. In research we would say the population
    of third graders in San Francisco is _____ (large/
    small).

■   large
■

8   In research we are seldom able to obtain measure-
    ments on every individual in a _____ .

■   population
■

9 When it is not feasible to measure every individual
   in a population, we may sample the population. If
   we measure the reading achievement of 100 third
   grade children in San Francisco, we have taken a
   _____ of the population of third grade children.

■
■ sample

10 A population always includes _____(all/some) of the
    individuals having its defining characteristics.

■
■ all

11 When we take a portion of a population with the de-
    fining characteristics, we have taken a _____ of
    the population.

■
■ sample

12 In research we are interested in individuals who
    have certain defining characteristics. Therefore, a
    sample will reflect the characteristics that define
    the _____ from which it was selected.

■
■ population

13 The purpose of research is to generalize about the
    behavior of a _____(sample/population).

■
■ population

14 In research in the behavioral sciences, the size of the population is generally _____(small/large).

■ large

15 Therefore, it is necessary to select a _____ (sample/population) in order to generalize to the _____ (sample/population).

■ sample, population

16 To generalize about the reading achievement of the population of third graders in a city your best estimate must be obtained from a _____ .

■ sample

17 To make accurate generalizations, it is necessary to obtain a representative sample of the _____ .

■ population

18 There are a number of factors that influence the validity of a generalization. In part, the validity of generalization depends on the size of the _____ .

■ sample

19 A sample of one individual _____(is/is not) likely to be representative of the _____ from which it is selected.

■ is not, population

20 Therefore, it would be risky to _____ to a
    population from a sample of one individual.

■ generalize

21 Usually, the larger the sample, the _____(more/
    less) likely it is to be representative of the popu-
    lation.

■ more

22 In most cases, if we randomly select a large sample,
    it _____(is/is not) likely to be representative
    of the population from which it was selected.

■ is

23 Thus, the most common procedure for obtaining a rep-
    resentative sample is _____ selection.

■ random

24 If we select a sample randomly, it is likely to be
    representative of the _____ .

■ population

25 The mean (average) reading score of a large random
    sample of third graders is likely to be _____
    of the population having these defining characteris-
    tics.

■ representative

26 Therefore, if the mean reading score of 100 randomly
    selected third graders in a city is 3.2, our best
    estimate of the mean score for the population of
    third graders for that city is _____ .

■
■ 3.2

27 If a sample is not randomly selected, it _____(is/
    is not) likely to be representative of the popula-
    tion.

■
■ is not

28 Third graders attending a demonstration school on a
    college campus in some city are not likely to be
    _____ of all third graders in that city.

■
■ representative

29 The demonstration school third graders are not like-
    ly to be representative because of selective factors
    that led to their school admission. Therefore, it
    would not be possible to _____ to the popula-
    tion of third graders in that city.

■
■ generalize

30 When a sample is not randomly selected, the chances
    that it is representative of the population are
    greatly _____(increased/reduced).

■
■ reduced

31 When a sample is not representative of a population,
    you should not _____ to the population.

■ generalize

32 Every element in the population must have an equal
    opportunity of being selected for the sample to be
    considered _____ .

■ random

33 In addition, the elements included in a sample must
    be independently selected. Thus, the selection of
    one element _____(must/must not) influence the
    selection of any other element.

■ must not

34 If we wish to generalize to all third graders in a
    city, then the sample of demonstration school third
    graders is an example of a _____ sample.

■ biased

35 Biased samples would _____(increase/decrease)
    the accuracy of generalizations regarding popula-
    tions.

■ decrease

36 If every element of a population does not have an equal opportunity of being selected, or elements have not been independently selected, it is termed a _____ sample.

■ biased

37 One method that may be used to insure that a sample is random is to use a table of random numbers. As the name implies, it is a table of numbers that have been selected _____ .

■ randomly

38 To use a table of random numbers it is first necessary to assign a number to every element in the _____ .

■ population

39 After assigning a number to each element in the population, the researcher makes a _____ selection from the array of numbers.

■ random

40 Table 1 (see page 89) contains numbers that are randomly selected, regardless of where we enter the table and regardless of what direction we read. Thus, we can start anywhere and move in any direction and be assured that the selection of numbers is _____ .

■ random

41 The following illustrates the use of the table of
   random numbers. Suppose the defining characteristics of a population were children in Ohio who had
   IQs of 150 and above, and there were only 42 such
   children in Ohio. The population would consist of
   _____ children.

■
■ 42

42 If we wished to select a sample of 12 children from
   this population, one method would be to use a table
   of _____ numbers.

■
■ random

43 To use this table, it is first necessary to assign a
   number to each individual (element) in the population. In the example, these numbers range from 01
   to _____ .

■
■ 42

44 Since we are concerned only with two-digit numbers,
   we will only be using _____ digits in the table of
   random numbers.

■
■ two

45 Suppose we arbitrarily decide to enter the table of
   random numbers at Row 00 and Columns 00 and 01. The
   first two digits of the number listed at this point
   in the table are _____ .

■
■ 23

46 Since 23 is the first number listed at the point where we entered the table, the first individual selected for the sample is the person who was assigned number ____ .

■
■ 23

47 If we decide to read straight down, the next three two-digit numbers listed are numbers ____ , ____ , and ____ .

■
■ 05, 14, 38

48 The next number listed is ____ which we ignore since the largest number assigned to an individual in our population is ____ .

■
■ 97, 42

49 Since the population consists of only 42 individuals, we ignore any number larger than ____ in the table of random numbers.

■
■ 42

50 We have now selected individuals with number 23, 05, 14, and 38. The next two-digit number between 1 and 42 appearing in the column is ____ .

■
■ 11

51 In this manner, we continue selecting individuals
    from the table of random numbers until we have ob-
    tained the designated number of ____ individuals to
    be included in the sample.

■ 12

52 Of course, when a number has been selected and
    appears again in the table, it _____(can/cannot)
    be selected again.

■ cannot

53 The 12 individuals selected from the population of
    42 are the individuals numbered 23, 05, 14, 38,

    ____ , ____ , ____ , ____ , ____ , ____ , ____ , and

    ____ .

■ 11, 36, 07, 31, 09, 25, 10, 37

54 As mentioned before, the table of random numbers may
    be entered at any point and numbers may be read in
    any prescribed _____ .

■ direction

TABLE 1   Table of Random Numbers

Row	Column Number
	00000
	01234
00	23157
01	05545
02	14871
03	38976
04	97312
05	11742
06	43361
07	93806
08	49540
09	36768
10	07092
11	43310
12	61570
13	31352
14	57048
15	09243
16	97957
17	93732
18	72621
19	61020
20	97839
21	89160
22	25966
23	81443
24	11322
25	64755
26	10302
27	71017
28	60012
29	37330
30	47869
31	38040
32	73508

8∎

STRATIFIED SAMPLING

1   One way of increasing the representativeness of a sample is to make certain that the elements included in the sample are selected in proportion to their occurrence in the _____ .

∎   population

2   When the elements in a sample are proportional to their presence in the population, the sample is said to be stratified. Thus, in addition to simple random sampling, another method of insuring representativeness is to obtain a _____ sample.

∎   stratified

3   For example, if age is considered an important determinant of opinions on educational issues, it would be important to discover the distribution of ages in the _____ .

∎   population

4   When we determine the distribution of ages, we have
    stratified the _____ on the characteristic of
    _____ .

■
■   population, age

5   One requirement for stratified sampling is that an
    element's membership in one stratum precludes its
    membership in any other stratum. For example, if we
    divide the population into high, middle, and low
    strata on socioeconomic status, an element could not
    appear in more than one _____ .

■
■   stratum

6   In stratified sampling, the population is divided in-
    to a number of strata, which _____(must/need
    not) be mutually exclusive.

■
■   must

7   Suppose we wish to obtain a stratified sample on the
    characteristic of sex and our population is 100
    tenth graders. They are divided by sex into strata
    containing 60 males and 40 females. For our sample,
    we should select males and females in the ratio of 6
    to ___ .

■
■   4

8   The male stratum contains ____ percent and the fe-
    male stratum contains ____ percent of the population.

■
■   60, 40

9 To determine the number of males to be selected, we
   should multiply the desired sample size by _____ .
   (Write your response as a decimal.)

■ .60

10 To determine the number of females to be selected,
   multiply the desired sample size by _____ . (Write
   your response as a decimal.)

■ .40

11 If we want a total sample of 20, we should select
   _____ males and ___ females.

■ 12, 8

12 The 12 males were obtained by multiplying 20 (the
   sample size) by _____ ; the 8 females were obtained
   by multiplying 20 (the sample size) by _____ .

■ .6, .4

13 In a sample, the representation of the elements in
   the strata is proportional to their representation
   in the _____ .

■ population

14 To insure maximal representativeness *within* a strata,
   the elements should be _____ selected.

■ randomly

15 In summary, when a population contains elements that are related to certain characteristics, such as age or socioeconomic status, the first step in selecting a representative sample is to determine the _____ of elements within each strata.

■ proportion

16 Then, within each stratum, the elements should be _____ selected.

■ randomly

STUDY 7-1

An administrator wishes to determine his teachers' reactions to a new educational program. He wishes to analyze their responses to a questionnaire according to the ages of the teachers, because their reactions may be influenced by their ages. The frequency distribution of the ages of the 488 teachers in his district is presented below:

Age	f
21-30	80
31-40	124
41-50	144
51-60	96
61-70	44
	$N = 488$

---

17 The administrator in Study 7-1 has _____ the
population of teachers on the characteristic of
_____ .

■ stratified, age

18 The population has been divided into _____ strata
of age.

■ five

19 Suppose the administrator wished to select a 25 percent sample from this population. The size of the
sample will be _____ .

■ 122

20 To insure that the sample is stratified on age, he
will need to take ____ percent of the teachers in
each _____ .

■ 25, stratum

21 The number of teachers in the population falling in
the 21-30 stratum is ____ .

■ 80

22 He needs to select 25 percent of the teachers in
each age stratum. Therefore, in the 21-30 stratum,
he must select ____ teachers.

■ 20

23 For a 25 percent sample, he must select 20 teachers
from the 21-30 stratum. The number of teachers to
be selected from each of the other strata are ____ ,
____ , ____ , and ____ .

■
■ 31, 36, 24, 11

24 Thus, by stratifying the population, it can be determined how many elements are to be sampled from each
stratum. To insure further that the sample is representative, the elements within each stratum must be
selected _____ .

■
■ randomly

25 Suppose the administrator wished to obtain a sample
of 75 teachers. He must select _____ percent of
this population.

■
■ 15.4

26 To obtain such a stratified sample from this population, he must select _____ percent of the teachers
within each _____ .

■
■ 15.4, stratum

27 Thus, we may obtain a stratified sample of a population by determining either (1) the percentage of the
_____ to be included in the sample, or (2)
the _____ size.

■
■ population, sample

28 The population in Study 7-1 was stratified on the one characteristic of _____ .

■ age

29 Of course it is possible to stratify a population on more than one _____ within the same study.

■ characteristic

STUDY 7-2

The principal of a junior high school wishes to determine the opinion of the student body regarding the types of desserts served in the school cafeteria. He feels that the opinions of boys and girls may differ, and also may differ among grade levels. The population of his school by age and grade level is given below:

Grade	Boys	Girls
seven	70	90
eight	50	70
nine	30	50

---

30 In Study 7-2 the population of the school consists of _____ students.

■ 360

31 If the principal thinks the opinions will differ be-
    tween the sexes and grades, to insure proportional
    representation of boys and girls within each grade
    level, he should obtain a _____ sample.

■ stratified

32 He should stratify the population on both the stu-
    dents' _____ and _____ .

■ sex, grade

33 The principal wishes to select a stratified sample
    of 90 students. This represents ____ percent of the
    population.

■ 25

34 This population is divided into _____ strata.

■ six

35 To obtain a stratified sample, he must take ____ per-
    cent of the students from each of the _____ strata.

■ 25, six

36 The number of seventh grade boys in the school popu-
    lation is ____ . The number of seventh grade boys
    to be included in his sample is _____ .

■ 70, 17.5

37 Of course, he cannot select exactly 17.5 boys. He
    must select either ____ or ____ .

■
■ 17, 18

38 To determine the complete stratified sample, he must
    determine how many students are to be included in
    each _____ .

■
■ stratum

39 Determine the number of students to be included in
    the 25 percent sample for each stratum.

Grade	Boys	Girls
seven	17.5	
eight		
nine		

17.5	22.5
12.5	17.5
7.5	12.5

40 To insure that his sample is representative, the
    school principal must _____ select students
    within each _____ .

■
■ randomly, stratum

98:

41 Suppose population is stratified into three strata—
    high, middle, and low intelligence. It is evident
    that the variability of intelligence in the total
    population is _____(greater/less) than the vari-
    ability within any particular stratum.

■ greater

42 Thus, when a population is stratified on some charac-
    teristic, the elements within each stratum are _____
    (more/less) homogeneous than are the elements within
    the entire population.

■ more

43 Assume that intelligence and reading ability are
    moderately correlated within a given population. In
    this case the more intelligent children generally
    are better _____.

■ readers

44 If we stratify the population on the characteristic
    of intelligence, we are, to some degree, also strati-
    fying it on the characteristic of _____ ability.

■ reading

45 If the population were stratified on intelligence,
    the individuals within each stratum of intelligence
    would be _____(more/less) homogeneous with respect
    to this characteristic than would be the elements
    within the _____ .

■ more, population

46   Further, if intelligence and reading ability are moderately correlated, stratification on the characteristic of intelligence would make the individuals more _____ on reading ability within each stratum.

■
■ homogeneous

47   If intelligence and reading ability were *perfectly* correlated, the individuals included in the stratum of "high" intelligence would be those included in the stratum of "high" _____ ability.

■
■ reading

48   Thus, in cases where two characteristics are perfectly correlated in the population, stratification on one characteristic would lead to perfect _____ on the other characteristic.

■
■ stratification

49   On the other hand, when two characteristics are only moderately correlated, stratification on one characteristic _____(will/will not) lead to perfect stratification on the other characteristic.

■
■ will not

50   However, if two characteristics are moderately correlated, stratification on one characteristic will have the effect of _____(increasing/reducing) the heterogeneity of the second characteristic within each stratum.

■
■ reducing

51 Although we may stratify a population on one charac-
    teristic, we should expect that the population
    _____(will/will not) vary on other characteris-
    tics.

■ will
■

PART

IV.

CONTROL OF EXTRANEOUS VARIABLES

Although the researcher's concern is focused on the effect of the independent variable, other variables may be responsible for producing changes in the dependent variable. The researcher may wish to control for independent variables by the process of randomization or by building control into the design of the study. The technical considerations for doing these are dealt with in Sets 9, 10, and 11.

The concept of "controlling for extraneous independent variables" and the rationale for doing so are set forth. Methods for "controlling" and their relationship to sampling and design are discussed. We will learn which method of control to use when we wish to obtain comparable groups without regard to an extraneous independent variable; which method to use when we are interested in analyzing changes in the dependent variable based on levels of an extraneous independent variable; and which method to use when there is a limited number of subjects available who have particular characteristics or when the manipulations to be introduced are extensive.

9∎

CONTROL BY RANDOMIZATION

1   "Children who have high self-concepts show greater
    gains in social studies achievement than children
    who have low self-concepts." The researcher hopes
    to be able to attribute gains in social studies
    achievement to the variable of self-concept rather
    than to some other _____ .

∎   variable

2   The independent variable is _____ and the
    dependent variable is _____ _____
    _____ .

∎   self-concept, social studies achievement

3   The researcher is interested in demonstrating the ef-
    fect of the _____(dependent/independent) var-
    iable on the _____ (dependent/independent)
    variable.

∎   independent, dependent

4 Now it may be that, in addition to self-concept, the gains in social studies achievement result from some other _____ .

■ variable

5 The only independent variable relevant to this investigation is _____ .

■ self-concept

6 Independent variables that are not related to the purpose of the study but may affect the dependent variable are termed extraneous variables. Because the researcher is concerned with the effect of self-concept on social studies achievement, intelligence would be considered a(n) _____ variable.

■ extraneous

7 A study must be designed in such a way as to make certain that the effect upon the dependent variable is attributed solely to the _____ variable, and not to some _____ variable or variables.

■ independent, extraneous

8 Thus, one requirement of good research design is to _____ (minimize/maximize) the influence or effect of extraneous variables.

■ minimize

9 We do not want changes in the dependent variable to result from extraneous variables but, rather, from the effects of the _____ variable.

▪ independent

10 Of course, we will be concerned with an extraneous variable only if it, in any way, is likely to affect the _____ variable.

▪ dependent

11 The technical term control is used when a study is designed to minimize the effects of extraneous variables. In frame 1, the researcher should _____ for the effects of intelligence.

▪ control

12 If the effect of intelligence on social studies achievement could be eliminated, the researcher would have controlled for the variable of _____ .

▪ intelligence

13 "Children exposed to reading method A (Group A) show greater gains in reading achievement than children exposed to reading method B (Group B)." The method of reading is the _____ variable.

▪ independent

14 The dependent variable is _____ _____
    scores.

■ reading achievement

15 Because intelligence affects reading scores, it can
    be considered an _____ variable in this study.

■ extraneous

16 If the children in Group A were on the average more
    intelligent than those in Group B, the greater gains
    in reading by Group A could result from the variable
    of _____ .

■ intelligence

17 Because we are interested in assessing the effects
    of the two methods of teaching reading, intelligence
    is considered a(n) _____ variable.

■ extraneous

18 To assess the effects of reading method on reading
    scores, we would need to _____ for the variable
    of intelligence.

■ control

19 One way of controlling for the variable of intelli-
    gence is to obtain two groups of children who are
    _____(comparable/different) on intelligence
    scores.

■
■   comparable

20 An extraneous variable not correlated with the de-
    pendent variable _____(could/could not) influ-
    ence it.

■
■   could not

21 We need to control for a variable if it is extrane-
    ous to the purposes of the study and _____(is/
    is not) correlated with the dependent variable.

■
■   is

22 If intelligence is not correlated with reading
    achievement, we _____(will/will not) need to
    control for the effects of intelligence.

■
■   will not

23 If the groups differ in intelligence, this variable
    would confound (make unclear) the effect of the read-
    ing methods on the gains in the _____ scores.

■
■   reading

24 When the dependent variable is not free from the influence of extraneous variables, the relationship between the dependent and independent variables is said to be _____ by an extraneous variable.

■
■ confounded

25 Confounding can be eliminated by _____ for the effect of extraneous variables.

■
■ controlling

26 We have learned that the random selection of individuals from a population permits us to obtain an unbiased and _____ sample.

■
■ representative

27 Of course, randomly selected individuals vary among themselves but in such a way that the total sample is usually representative of the _____ .

■
■ population

28 If you randomly assign individuals to Group A and to Group B, it is likely that the two groups _____ (would/would not) be comparable on most variables.

■
■ would

29 Thus, at the beginning of the study in frame 13, the
    two randomly assigned groups are likely to be
    _____ on the dependent variable of _____
    _____ .

■
■ comparable, reading achievement

30 If individuals are selected randomly, the two groups
    _____ (are/are not) likely to be comparable on
    such extraneous variables as intelligence.

■
■ are

31 By randomly assigning individuals to the two groups,
    the groups are likely to be comparable at the start
    of the study on the dependent variable as well as on
    _____ variables.

■
■ extraneous

32 By the random assignment of individuals to the
    groups, we have _____ for the effects of the
    extraneous variable intelligence.

■
■ controlled

33 If the individuals in the two groups are comparable
    on intelligence and Group A shows greater gains in
    reading scores than Group B, we know that the gains
    do not result from the variable of _____ .

■
■ intelligence

34 That is, the gains in reading are not _____
    by the extraneous variable of intelligence.

■ confounded
■

35 Of course, intelligence may not be the only extrane-
    ous variable related to the dependent variable. But
    if we have randomly selected a large enough sample,
    we can be relatively safe in assuming that we have
    _____ for all extraneous variables.

■ controlled
■

36 The process of randomization reduces the probability
    of _____ variables having a differential ef-
    fect on the study groups.

■ extraneous
■

37 In some investigations, it is impossible to control
    for the effect of extraneous variables by randomly
    selecting individuals for the groups. For example,
    suppose Mrs. Jones' class receives method A and Mrs.
    Smith's class receives method B. If Mrs. Jones'
    class has a higher intelligence level, we have not
    been able to control intelligence by _____ selec-
    tion.

■ random
■

38 If we cannot control for the effect of extraneous variables by random selection, there are statistical techniques that permit us to assess the effect of the independent variable on the dependent variable, taking into account the influence of _____ variables.

■■ extraneous

39 Thus, there are techniques that permit us to control statistically for the effects of extraneous variables in cases where we cannot control such variables by _____ selection.

■■ random

40 Suppose Mrs. Jones' class (which is the more intelligent) showed greater gains in reading achievement after receiving method A than did Mrs. Smith's class after receiving method B. If we know there is a correlation between intelligence and gains in reading scores, we can attribute some of the differential gain in reading to the variable of _____ .

■■ intelligence

41 Then, the question is, "Does the greater gain exhibited by Mrs. Jones' class result from the extraneous variable of _____ or from the independent variable of _____ _____ , or from some of both?"

■■ intelligence, reading method

SET

10∎

CONTROL BY HOMOGENEITY

1 It is not always possible to control extraneous variables by randomization. If there are differences between groups chosen at random, the effects of extraneous variables could be attributed to _____ (nonchance/chance) factors.

∎ chance

2 The researcher in the behavioral sciences frequently must work with intact (established) groups. Because selective factors may play a major role in the determination of intact groups, it is likely that groups would differ on independent variables that are _____ to the study.

∎ extraneous

3 If comparability by randomization is not possible, other methods must be found to _____ for the effects of extraneous variables.

∎ control

113:

4   The term "control" means "eliminate the effects of
    extraneous variables." However, this is not to be
    taken literally because an extraneous variable will
    continue to affect the _____ variable, if cor-
    related with it.

■
■   dependent

5   "Control," in the sense used in research, implies
    that groups have been made comparable on one or
    more _____ variables.

■
■   extraneous

6   Making groups comparable on extraneous variables
    _____ (increases/decreases) the differential ef-
    fect of such variables on the groups being studied.

■
■   decreases

7   We should attempt to obtain groups that are compara-
    ble on extraneous variables if these variables are
    correlated with the _____ variable.

■
■   dependent

8   Controlling for an extraneous variable does not re-
    move the correlation between it and the dependent
    variable. The differential effects of the extrane-
    ous variable have been removed, thus making the
    groups _____ on this variable.

■
■   comparable

9 If we control for IQ for two groups being exposed to different reading methods, we _____ (have/ have not) made the groups comparable on IQ.

■ have

10 Controlling for IQ _____ (does/does not) mean that IQ will no longer affect the dependent variable.

■ does not

11 For example, if the correlation between IQ and reading is positive, and we controlled for IQ, we _____ (would/would not) eliminate the correlation between IQ and reading.

■ would not

12 However, after controlling for IQ, this extraneous variable _____ (would/would not) have a differential effect on reading for the groups being compared.

■ would not

13 The purpose of controlling for extraneous variables is to make groups _____ on these variables.

■ comparable

14 The term used for eliminating the differential effects of variables extraneous to the purpose of the
study is "_____ ."

■
■ control

15 Besides randomization, one method for making groups
comparable on an extraneous variable is to select
samples that are as _____ (homogeneous/
heterogeneous) as possible on that variable.

■
■ homogeneous

16 If we selected only children who were eight years of
age for our study, we would _____ (decrease/in-
crease) the likely effects of age on the dependent
variable.

■
■ decrease

17 By selecting only eight-year-old children, we have
_____ for the effects of age as an extraneous
independent variable.

■
■ controlled

18 Thus, one method for removing the effects of intelligence on the dependent variable is to select a
_____ (wide/restricted) range of intellectual
ability.

■
■ restricted

19 By selecting a restricted range of ability on an in-
    dependent variable, we make the population more
    _____ (homogeneous/heterogeneous) on that
    variable.

■ homogeneous

20 If we restricted the population to children with IQs
    between 120 and 139, we have _____ for the ef-
    fects of IQ.

■ controlled

21 Even though we have some variability within the IQ
    range of 120-139, the likely effects of IQ within
    this group on the dependent variable would be _____
    (small/great).

■ small

22 If we further reduced the IQ range, we would further
    _____ (reduce/increase) the effects of IQ on the
    dependent variable.

■ reduce

23 In fact, if we had selected only individuals whose
    IQ scores were 120, we could not explain differences
    on the dependent variable in terms of ____ scores.

■ IQ

24 When all individuals have identical scores on some variable, we have attained maximal _____ of the effects of that variable on the dependent variable.

■ control

25 We would be concerned with controlling for the effects of an extraneous variable only if it _____ (is/is not) correlated with the _____ (independent/dependent) variable.

■ is, dependent

26 When an extraneous independent variable is correlated with the dependent variable, it is possible to control for that independent variable by making the population _____ on that variable.

■ homogeneous

27 If we randomly assigned individuals to reading methods A and B from a highly homogeneous population of IQ scores, the two groups are virtually certain to be _____ (comparable/different) on IQ.

■ comparable

28 If we compared reading methods A and B for children in the IQ range of 120-139, you _____ (could/could not) generalize to children below this IQ range regarding the relative effectiveness of these two reading methods.

■ could not

29 Selecting a sample from a homogeneous population
    _____(increases/decreases) the generalizabil-
    ity of the findings.

■ decreases

30 Comparing homogeneous groups limits the
    _____ of the findings.

■ generalizability

31 To determine whether the findings for the IQ range
    of 120-139 would hold for other IQ ranges, we could
    conduct a series of separate studies. In this case
    we would _____ for the effects of different IQ
    strata one at a time.

■ control

32 A more efficient research design is to analyze the
    effects of reading methods A and B for different IQ
    ranges within the same study by establishing
    _____(homogeneous/heterogeneous) categories
    of IQ.

■ homogeneous

```
┌─────────────────────────────────────────────────────────┐
│                                                           │
│  EXAMPLE 10-1                                             │
│                                                           │
│         Mean Reading Achievement Scores                   │
│         ─────────────────────────────────────────        │
│         IQ Stratum          Reading  Method               │
│                                A        B                 │
│         ─────────────────────────────────────────        │
│         High (> 115)          65       64                 │
│         Middle (86-114)       56       59                 │
│         Low (< 85)            44       33                 │
│         ─────────────────────────────────────────        │
│                                                           │
└─────────────────────────────────────────────────────────┘
```

33 Example 10-1 presents the mean reading scores for
the two reading methods, A and B, for the three IQ
strata of _____ , _____ . and _____ .

■ high, middle, low

34 Although the designation of high, middle, and low IQ
is arbitrary, each stratum is more _____
(homogeneous/heterogeneous) than the total IQ range.

■ homogeneous

35 From inspection, it would appear that reading methods A and B clearly differ in effectiveness only for
the _____ IQ stratum.

■ low

36 Had we controlled for the effects of the extraneous
    variable—IQ—by randomization rather than by homo-
    geneity, we _____(would/would not) have been
    able to determine that reading methods differ in ef-
    fectiveness for different IQ strata.

■
■   would not

37 Thus, in one design, the definitiveness of the study
    has been enhanced by using homogeneous strata of IQ.
    In effect, we have determined the differential ef-
    fect of the _____ variable on the _____
    variable for various IQ strata.

■
■   independent, dependent

38 In one experiment, we were able to compare two read-
    ing methods for different strata of IQ, thereby in-
    creasing the efficiency of the research and permit-
    ting us to _____ to a much larger population.

■
■   generalize

39 Each IQ stratum is relatively homogeneous and, there-
    fore, IQ is _____ .

■
■   controlled

40 That is, the difference in the reading scores for
    methods A and B for the low IQ stratum is not con-
    founded by the _____ of the children.

■
■   intelligence

41 It is possible that an extraneous independent variable other than IQ could have _____ the relationship between the independent and dependent variables.

■
■ confounded

42 For example, if reading achievement were related to
the sex of the children, the difference between the
two methods for the low IQ stratum could be attributed to differences in _____ .

■
■ sex

43 Thus, sex would be an additional extraneous variable
that should be _____ by homogeneity.

■
■ controlled

44 Therefore, it is sometimes necessary to control for
more than one _____ independent variable within the same study.

■
■ extraneous

45 If we believed that reading scores might be affected
not only by IQ but by sex as well, we should have a
sufficiently large number of children so that they
can be divided into groups of _____ and _____
within each IQ stratum.

■
■ males, females

```
┌─────────────────────────────────────────────────────────────┐
│                                                               │
│   EXAMPLE 10-2                                                 │
│                                                               │
│          Mean Reading Achievement Scores                      │
│      ─────────────────────────────────────────────           │
│               Reading Method A     Reading Method B           │
│                                                               │
│   IQ Stratum   Males    Females    Males    Females           │
│      ─────────────────────────────────────────────           │
│   High          64        66        65        65              │
│   Middle        57        56        59        57              │
│   Low           48        40        37        29              │
│      ─────────────────────────────────────────────           │
│                                                               │
└─────────────────────────────────────────────────────────────┘
```

46 Example 10-2 presents the mean reading scores for a
    sample that has been stratified by _____
    and _____ for each reading method.

■
■ intelligence, sex

47 Whereas in Example 10-1 we were able to analyze the
    data only for different IQ strata, in Example 10-2
    we can analyze these data by the _____ of the chil-
    dren as well.

■
■ sex

48 It is evident that, regardless of the reading method
    or sex of the children, the mean reading scores
    _____(are/are not) related to the children's in-
    telligence.

■
■ are

49 For high IQ males, it appears that the two reading
    methods are _____(equally/differentially)
    effective.

■ equally

50 Therefore, we can conclude that both reading methods
    are equally effective for high IQ males. From the
    data, it is probable that a similar statement can be
    made for high IQ _____ .

■ females

51 It appears that reading methods A and B for the mid-
    dle IQ stratum probably are _____(equally/
    differentially) effective, regardless of sex.

■ equally

52 For the low IQ stratum, the effectiveness of the two
    reading methods appears to be _____(equal/
    different).

■ different

53 Further, for the low IQ stratum, there appears to be
    a difference in the effectiveness of the two reading
    methods based on the _____ of the children.

■ sex

54 By stratifying the sample by sex and IQ, the definitiveness of the findings has been _____ (in-
creased/decreased).

■ increased

11.

CONTROL BY MATCHING[1]

1 A study has been designed to compare the relative effectiveness of extensive individual counseling and
group counseling on changes in students' ego
strength. Thirty high school freshmen who have not
yet had counseling are selected for this study. The
type of counseling is the _____ variable,
and ego strength is the _____ variable.

■
■ independent, dependent

2 Previous research has shown that scholastic achievement is correlated with ego strength. If achievement is extraneous to the purposes of this study, we
should _____ for the effects of this variable.

■ control

-----

[1] This procedure is sometimes referred to as "block-
ing."

3   It is desirable to have maximal control of the stu-
    dent's achievement so changes in ego development can
    be explained as a result of _____ rather than
    achievement.

■
■   counseling

4   Because of the extensiveness of the counseling ses-
    sions, we will not have a sufficiently large sample
    to stratify the children into levels of
    _____ .

■
■   achievement

5   Of course, achievement may not be the only extrane-
    ous variable correlated with the _____ varia-
    ble.

■
■   dependent

6   Any variable that is _____ with the _____
    variable will need to be controlled for.

■
■   correlated, dependent

7   To allow for maximal generalizability, we will need
    to sample from a _____ (homogeneous/hetero-
    geneous) population of student achievement scores.

■
■   heterogeneous

8 If the study is restricted to "high" achievers, we
   limit the _____ of the findings.

■ generalizability

9 The assumption that randomization has controlled for
   the effects of extraneous variables is risky in
   studies of _____(small/large) samples.

■ small

10 Because the counseling groups would each contain
   only 15 children, the control of extraneous variables by randomization _____(would/would not)
   be a good technique.

■ would not

11 One procedure for gaining control of the variables
   of achievement is to match individuals so that each
   pair of individuals is as _____(comparable/
   unlike) as possible.

■ comparable

12 Thus, matching requires that pairs of _____
   (individuals/groups) be identified who are highly
   similar on the variable to be controlled.

■ individuals

13 For example, two individuals whose overall grade
point average is 3.5 can be said to be _____
on achievement.

■ matched

EXAMPLE 11-1 Matching by Achievement

Group Counseling (GC)	Individual Counseling (IC)	Freshman Student Number	GPA
	X←	①	3.86
X←		②	3.84
	X←	③	3.79
X←		④	3.76
	X←	⑤	3.57
X←		⑥	3.55
		7	3.34
		8	3.31
		9	3.23
		10	3.20
		29	1.13
		30	1.08

14 Example 11-1 contains the grade point average (GPA)
for 30 randomly selected high school freshmen. One
limitation on the generalizability of the findings
is that all of the subjects are _____ _____
_____ .

■ high school freshmen

15 However, because the subjects are randomly selected, we can assume they are _____ of the population of freshmen from their particular high school.

■ representative

16 To obtain matched pairs, we must first rank order the students on the variable of _____ _____ _____ _____.

■ grade point average/achievement

17 GPA has been rank ordered with the highest score at the _____ (top/bottom).

■ top

18 The first two students constitute the first pair. The GPAs of the first matched pair are _____ and _____.

■ 3.86, 3.84

19 One student of this matched pair will be assigned to individual counseling and the other student to _____ _____.

■ group counseling

20 To prevent bias in the assignment of students to individual and group counseling, it would be best to assign the students from each matched pair _____.

■ randomly

21 However, for ease of illustration in Example 11-1, systematic assignment has been carried out. The odd numbered students are assigned to ____ (IC/GC) and the even numbered students to ____ (IC/GC).

■ IC, GC

22 The assignment of student No. 1 to either IC or GC was determined by the flip of a coin. On the basis of this flip, student No. 1 was assigned to the ____ (GC/IC) group.

■ IC

23 Because the GPAs are relatively similar for each pair, it is likely that the GPAs of the IC and GC groups will be _____ (comparable/incomparable).

■ comparable

24 However, the second score in each matched pair is somewhat _____ (higher/lower) than the first score.

■ lower

25 The mean of GPAs of the students in the ____ (IC/GC) group will be somewhat lower than those in the ____ (IC/GC) group.

■ GC, IC

26 One way to compensate for this slight bias is to have the first student of each succeeding matched pair assigned _____(systematically/ alternately) to IC and GC.

■ alternately

27 If we alternated the assignment of the first student of each pair, the students in IC for the first five matched pairs would be ___ , ___ , ___ , ___ , ___ .

■ 1, 4, 5, 8, 9

28 To check on the degree to which the procedure of assigning the first student of each pair alternately to IC and GC has increased the comparability on GPA of these two groups, enter the GPA scores in the following tables.

Procedure I				Procedure II			
IC		GC		IC		GC	
Student	GPA	Student	GPA	Student	GPA	Student	GPA
1	___	2	___	1	___	2	___
3	___	4	___	4	___	3	___
5	___	6	___	5	___	6	___
7	___	8	___	8	___	7	___
9	___	10	___	9	___	10	___

Procedure I				Procedure II			
IC		GC		IC		GC	
Student	GPA	Student	GPA	Student	GPA	Student	GPA
1	3.86	2	3.84	1	3.86	2	3.84
3	3.79	4	3.76	4	3.76	3	3.79
5	3.57	6	3.55	5	3.57	6	3.55
7	3.34	8	3.31	8	3.31	7	3.34
9	3.23	10	3.20	9	3.23	10	3.20

29 The sums of the GPAs for Procedure I are: IC _____ ,
GC _____ .

■ 17.79, 17.66

30 The sums of the GPAs for Procedure II are:
IC _____ , GC _____ .

■ 17.73, 17.72

31 Of course, any systematic bias can be eliminated by
_____ assigning students from each matched pair
to IC and GC.

■ randomly

32 In the previous study the students were matched on
GPA. Had the researcher not been able to use randomization in the assignment of students to the types
of counseling, the matching procedure _____
(would/would not) adequately control for the effects
of other extraneous variables.

■ would not

PART

INTERNAL AND EXTERNAL VALIDITY OF RESEARCH FINDINGS

The concern of hypothesis-testing research is with
the effect of a manipulated or nonmanipulated independent variable. In Part 4 of the text, the importance of controlling for extraneous variables was
stressed. Set 12 of Part 5 on internal validity
elaborates the factors that may confound the interpretation of the effects of an independent variable.
Threats to the internal validity of a study pose
problems with respect to the interpretation of the
effects of the independent variable on the dependent
variable. Set 12 presents threats to internal validity from selection, history, maturation, testing
effect, reactive measures, instrumentation effects,[1]
statistical regression, and experimental mortality.
   A number of factors may threaten the extent to
which the findings of a study may be generalized to
other populations or conditions. These threats
relate to the external validity of a study and are

[1] The authors wish to express their gratitude to
D. T. Campbell and J. C. Stanley for their exposi-
tion of threats to internal and external validity.
See Campbell and Stanley, "Experimental and quasi-
experimental designs for research on teaching." In
N. L. Gage (ed.), *Handbook of Research on Teaching*.
Chicago: Rand-McNally, 1963, Chapter 5.

135:

essentially a concern with the representativeness of
the research findings. Set 13 presents threats to
external validity from the interaction of selection
and treatment, pretest sensitization, the reactive effect of treatments, and multiple treatment interference.

12∎

INTERNAL VALIDITY

1 In Part 4 we learned that we must eliminate, or at least minimize, the effects of extraneous variables on the _____ variable.

∎ dependent

2 We need to carry out our experiment in a way that controls for the effects of _____ variables.

∎ extraneous

3 Thus, we wish to control the extraneous variables so as to reduce the confounding of their effects with the effects of the _____ variable(s) in the study.

∎ independent

4 For a study to have *internal validity* it must adequately control for the effects of _____ variables.

■ extraneous

5 To the extent that the effects of extraneous variables are removed or reduced, the internal validity of a study is _____ (increased/decreased).

■ increased

6 A study that controls extraneous variables permits the researcher to attribute changes in the dependent variable to the effects of the independent variable with _____ (greater/lesser) accuracy.

■ greater

7 Thus, the essential consideration in determining the worth of a study is its _____ validity.

■ internal

8 If there is bias in the selection and assignment of subjects to comparison groups, this could adversely affect the _____ validity of the study.

■ internal

9   Thus, one factor that poses a threat to the internal
    validity of a study is the manner in which the sub-
    jects are _____ and assigned to groups.

■
■   selected

10 Any bias that enters into the composition of compari-
    son groups _____ (will/will not) threaten the
    _____ validity of a study.

■
■   will, internal

11 That is, a biased selection of samples may affect
    the outcome of the study so that we would be unable
    to conclude whether the effect on the dependent vari-
    able resulted from the _____ variable or
    from the _____ selection procedures.

■
■   independent, sample

12 Comparing groups that had been self-selected
    _____ (would/would not) control for the effects
    of extraneous variables.

■
■   would not

13 For example, volunteers are likely to represent a(n)
    _____ (biased/unbiased) sample.

■
■   biased

14 Thus, comparing volunteers with nonvolunteers represents a threat to the _____ _____ of a
study.

■
■ internal validity

15 As discussed earlier, a powerful procedure for controlling the effect of extraneous independent variables is the _____ assignment of subjects to experimental and control groups.

■
■ random

16 Although group equality is not assured by the random
assignment of subjects, such assignment yields
_____(biased/unbiased) samples.

■
■ unbiased

17 If a group of volunteers exposed to some experimental program evidenced greater competence at the conclusion of the program than nonvolunteers, it
_____(would/would not) be safe to assume that
the difference between the groups resulted from the
experimental program.

■
■ would not

18 To accept the difference as resulting from the independent variable, it would be necessary to show that
the volunteer and nonvolunteer groups were initially
comparable on the _____ variable.

■
■ dependent

19 In addition, we would also need to assume that the two groups were comparable on all other variables that might affect the _____ variable.

■ dependent

20 In general, if a researcher can demonstrate that difference(s) in the dependent variable(s) result(s) from the effects of some experimental intervention (independent variable) rather than from uncontrolled factors, we can conclude that the study has _____ _____ .

■ internal validity

21 We have shown that the differential *selection* of subjects for experimental and control groups may threaten the internal validity of a study. Other factors may also affect internal validity. The term *history* is used to refer to the environmental events occurring during a study that may affect the subjects in the study. The history of all subjects _____(is/ is not) likely to be identical during the study.

■ is not

22 The longer the period for which a study is conducted, the _____(less/more) likely is such differential exposure to occur.

■ more

23 A history of absences due to unanticipated prolonged illnesses of a number of experimental group subjects during a study should be considered as a threat to the _____ _____ of the study.

∎ internal validity

24 Given such absences, the lack of differences between experimental and control groups on the dependent variable might be plausibly attributed to the effects of differential _____ in school attendance.

∎ histories

25 Apart from the independent variable, it is desirable that experimental and control groups do not differ markedly with regard to their _____ during the study.

∎ histories

26 Another factor that may threaten the internal validity of a study is *maturation*. Maturation is defined as the changes that take place in subjects over time. As with history, maturation _____ (is/is not) likely to be similar for all subjects over time.

∎ is not

27 Developmental changes, whether physical or psychological, would be examples of the effects of _____ (history/maturation).

∎ maturation

28 Differential changes in growth rates between experimental and control subjects would confound the effects of the independent variable, thus posing a
threat to the _____._____ of the study.

■ internal validity

29 Maturation refers to both physical and psychological
changes. An increase in body size is an example of
_____ maturation. An increase in motivation of
subjects is an example of _____ maturation.

■ physical, psychological

30 Therefore, maturation must be thought of as refer-
ring to _____ and/or _____ factors.

■ physical, psychological

31 Although the term maturation implies growth, growth
can refer to negative effects. For example, growing
bored is a negative _____ effect.

■ maturational

32 If increased boredom was produced in the experimental subjects during the period of a study, this maturational effect may _____ (enhance/reduce) the effects of an independent variable.

■ reduce

33 In general, the longer the time period of a study, the _____ (more/less) are maturational effects likely to reduce the internal validity of the study.

■ more
■

34 Equating comparison groups will help to _____ for the effects of maturation.

■ control
■

35 Many research studies pretest the subjects before the independent variable is introduced. It is conceivable that taking a pretest may influence how the subjects respond on the _____ test.

■ post
■

36 The effect of pretesting on the subjects' posttest scores is referred to as the *testing* effect. This testing effect is usually not a part of the treatment (independent variable) and thus it poses another threat to the _____ validity of the study.

■ internal
■

37 It is possible for subjects to "change" as a result of taking a pretest. The effects of the independent variable on the posttest scores would be confounded by the effects of _____ .

■ testing
■

38 The nature of the pretest and the conditions under which it is given will determine its impact on the _____ .

■■ posttest

39 When a posttest is administered shortly after the pretest, the effects of memory would be _____ (less/greater) than if the posttest is administered after a longer interval.

■■ greater

40 The greater the individual's reactions to a pretest and the more obtrusive the pretest, the greater is the likelihood that _____ _____ will be reduced.

■■ internal validity

41 For example, if a pretest contains items that are embarrassing to the subject, taking the pretest _____ (is/is not) likely to affect the way in which the subject responds to the same items on the posttest.

■■ is

42 Compared with a test item assessing mathematic ability, an item dealing with social attitudes is _____ (more/less) likely to evoke a socially desirable response.

■■ more

43 Test situations in which the socially desirable re-
    sponses are obvious will tend to _____ (increase/
    decrease) the internal validity of a study.

■ decrease

44 Anonymity is likely to _____ (reduce/increase)
    the probability that the individual will select re-
    sponses that put him or her in a favorable light.

■ reduce

45 Thus, in attitude studies, anonymity is likely to re-
    duce the effect of the _____ on the posttest and
    thereby _____ (increase/decrease) the internal
    validity of the study.

■ pretest, increase

46 If the manner in which measurements are obtained on
    the dependent variable undergoes change during the
    course of the study, such change may result in dif-
    ferences between the _____ - and _____ test scores.

■ pre, post

47 The effects of changes in the data gathering proce-
    dures are termed *instrumentation effects*. Pretest-
    posttest differences from instrumentation effects
    _____ (are/are not) presumed to be part of the ef-
    fects of the independent variable.

■ are not

48 Because such effects may result in differences be-
    tween the pretest and posttest scores, instrumenta-
    tion effects are a threat to the _____ validity
    of a study.

■
■   internal

49 There are a number of ways in which instrumentation
    effects can occur. If mechanical devices are used
    to obtain measurements on the dependent variable, it
    is possible that the device will not perform con-
    sistently over a period of time because of constant
    use. Such instrument decay may produce differences
    between the _____ - and _____ test scores.

■
■   pre, post

50 Since differences obtained as a result of instrument
    decay _____(do/do not) result from the effects of
    the independent variable, such effects are a threat
    to the _____ _____ of the study.

■
■   do not, internal validity

51 Similarly, if there is a difference in the fatigue
    level of observers from pre to post observations,
    this would be termed an _____ effect.

■
■   instrumentation

52 If judges, interviewers, or observers improve their measurement skills during the course of the study, such improvement _____ (would/would not) affect the differences between pretest and posttest measurements. This _____ (would/would not) threaten the internal validity of the study.

■ would, would

53 Informing observers about the purpose of a study may bias their judgment and thus _____(increase/ decrease) the internal validity of the study.

■ decrease

54 Knowledge of which subjects are in the experimental and control groups may bias the data gathering process. For example, the tester may show less enthusiasm toward the control group and this may differentially affect the data obtained for the two groups. Thus, any measured difference between the experimental and control groups could result from _____ effects and not from the effects of the _____ variable.

■ instrumentation, independent

55 Randomizing the experimental and control subjects for obtaining measurements on the dependent variable and not informing the tester which subjects belong to the experimental and control groups would _____(increase/decrease) instrumentation effects and thus increase the _____ _____ of the study.

■ decrease, internal validity

56 Any changes in the method for obtaining data during the course of a study, whether from instrument decay, observer fatigue, bias, or improved skill, are called _____ effects and are a threat to the internal validity of the study because they may produce results that do not result from the _____ variable.

∎ instrumentation, independent

57 A high degree of standardization of the procedures used for data gathering will _____(increase/ decrease) the likelihood of instrumentation effects.

∎ decrease

58 Instrumentation effects and testing effects are different in that the instrumentation effects occur as a result of changes in the _____ (data gathering procedures/study subjects), whereas testing effects occurs as a result of changes in the _____(data gathering procedures/ study subjects) because of pretesting.

∎ data gathering procedures, study subjects

59 If the experimental subjects were tested individually and the control subjects were tested as a group for both the pretests and posttests, the internal validity would be threatened because of _____(history/instrumentation/testing) effect.

∎ instrumentation

60 If the control group had a change in teachers during the study, the internal validity would be threatened because of _____ (history/instrumentation/ testing) effect.

∎ history

61 If the experimental group exhibited a gain from pre-test to posttest because they learned from the pre-test, the internal validity would be threatened be-cause of _____ (history/instrumentation/ testing) effect.

∎ testing

62 Another potential threat to the internal validity of a study, called *statistical regression,* may be pre-sent in studies where the sample of subjects is se-lected because they have extreme pretest scores on the dependent variable. For example, if an experi-mental group is composed of subjects who have been selected because they have the lowest scores on an arithmetic achievement test (dependent variable), this would be considered an extreme group. If the highest scorers had been chosen as the sample, this also would be termed a(n) _____ group.

∎ extreme

63 For such extreme scoring samples, statistical regres-sion occurs because of the unreliability of the measuring instrument. To be maximally useful, the measuring instrument should provide accurate measure-ments; that is, the test scores must be _____ .

∎ reliable

64 Although in the behavioral sciences, the reliability of measuring instruments tends to be fairly high, they are not perfect (the correlation coefficient is not +1.00). That is, the obtained measurements are not perfectly _____ .

■ reliable

65 Regression effect is defined as the tendency for in- dividuals or groups selected on the basis of extreme scores to "move closer" on retesting to the mean of the population from which they were selected. As can be expected, this effect is more pronounced for tests of _____(low/high) reliability.

■ low

66 The higher the reliability coefficient for the de- pendent variable, the _____(less/greater) the statistical regression.

■ less

67 In effect, a perfectly reliable test would evidence no _____ _____ .

■ statistical regression

68 Were the reliability of a test to be zero, the amount of regression would be _____(minimal/ maximal).

■ maximal

69 Statistical regression represents a threat to the internal validity of a study if samples have been chosen on the basis of extreme scores using an instrument that has less-than-perfect _____ .

■ reliability

70 For example, suppose a sample of students had been selected because it represented the highest scorers on a spelling achievement test. The mean spelling achievement score for this sample was 120. If the measurements obtained on this test are not perfectly reliable, upon retesting the sample would have a _____ (lower/higher) mean score.

■ lower

71 On the other hand, if the sample was composed of low-scoring students, having a spelling achievement test mean score of 75, upon retesting the mean score of this sample would be _____ (lower/higher) than 75.

■ higher

72 Were we to select a sample having scores which were even more extreme the statistical regression would be _____ (less/greater).

■ greater

73 Maximal regression, then, would be shown by the _____ (most/least) extreme scores.

■ most

74 The statistical regression effect shows the influence of errors of measurement. The magnitude of
the errors of measurement of a test is reflected in
its reliability coefficient. The higher the reliability coefficient the _____(smaller/greater)
the errors of measurement.

■ smaller

75 Errors of measurement in the population are random
and tend to cancel themselves out. That is, in the
population there _____(are/are not) likely to
be as many negative errors (errors that reduce the
score) as positive errors (errors that increase the
score).

■ are

76 However, the further an individual's score or a
group's mean score is from the mean of the population from which it was selected the more likely are
such scores to contain differential errors of measurement. That is, for high scoring subjects, these
errors of measurement are more likely to be
_____(positive/negative) errors and for low
scoring subjects these errors are more likely to be
_____(positive/negative) errors.

■ positive, negative

77 Since one type of error of measurement occurs when
subjects guess while taking a test, it is logical to
assume that high scorers on a pretest are probably
"guessing lucky." It _____(is/is not) likely
that they would be as lucky on retesting.

■ is not

78 Therefore, their scores on retest would be _____
        _____ (higher than/the same as/lower than) they
    were on the pretest.

■ lower than

79 If negative errors of measurement have affected the
    pretest scores of low-scoring subjects, their post-
    test scores _____ (are/are not) likely to be simi-
    larly affected.

■ are not

80 In effect, subjects selected for their low scores on
    the pretest, will show _____ (higher/lower) scores
    on the posttest, because of statistical regression.

■ higher

81 Similarly, for subjects selected for their high
    scores on the pretest their scores will move
    _____ (toward/away from) the mean of the popula-
    tion from which they were chosen.

■ toward

82 Such high-scoring individuals on the pretest are
    likely to evidence _____ (higher/lower) scores on
    the posttest, because of statistical regression.

■ lower

83   The technical term for the phenomenon of individual
     or group scores moving toward the mean of the popula-
     tion from which they were selected, is statistical
     _____ .

■   regression

84   Statistical regression effects can result in differ-
     ences between pretest and posttest scores of extreme
     groups that _____(do/do not) result from the inde-
     pendent variable.

■   do not

85   Because of the confounding of the statistical regres-
     sion effects with the effects of the independent var-
     iable, statistical regression is a threat to the
     _____ _____ of a study where samples have
     been selected on the basis of _____ pretest
     scores.

■   internal validity, extreme

86   Studies conducted over time may evidence a loss of
     subjects, which is technically known as *experimental
     mortality*. If such loss is differential for the con-
     trol and experimental groups, differences between
     their posttest scores _____(are/are not) likely
     to be confounded.

■   are

87 If some individuals are inaccessible for posttesting
    because they are ill or have moved from the area,
    this _____ (will/will not) result in experimen-
    tal mortality.

■ will

88 The refusal of some subjects to continue in the re-
    search _____ (is/is not) an example of experimen-
    tal mortality.

■ is

89 Although two groups may have been randomly selected
    and assigned to the experimental and control groups,
    selective loss in one or the other group may con-
    found the interpretation of the findings because of

    _____ _____ .

■ experimental mortality

90 The differential histories of subjects who remain in
    the study _____ (is/is not) an example of experi-
    mental mortality.

■ is not

91 Experimental mortality may occur selectively between
    experimental and control groups and therefore may af-
    fect the _____ _____ of the study.

■ internal validity

92 Of course, it is possible for two or more factors affecting internal validity to have a joint or inter-
active effect on the scores of the _____ variable.

■
■ dependent

93 In particular, interaction effects may occur in con-
junction with the differential selection of study
subjects. Such interaction effects may be mistaken
for the effect of the independent variable, thus affecting the _____ _____ of the study.

■
■ internal validity

94 One group in a study may differ not only with respect to the dependent variable, or other relevant
variables, but also with respect to their history
during the study. The combined selection-history effect is an example of _____ effects.

■
■ interaction

95 Selection effects may operate jointly with maturation. For example, one group may mature more rapid-
ly than the other study group. In this instance,
the interaction between selection and maturation
will operate to confound the effects of the
_____ variable on the _____ variable.

■
■ independent, dependent

96 Any factor or combination of factors that may confound the interpretation of the effects of the independent variable on the dependent variable are considered threats to the _____ _____ of a
study.

■ internal validity

13:

EXTERNAL VALIDITY

1 Although the internal validity of a study is of primary importance for the unambiguous interpretation
of the effects of the independent variable, a second
criterion for judging a study is its external

_____ .

■ validity

2 Of concern here is the answer to the question: Are
the findings of a study representative of what can
be expected for other populations, conditions, and
criterion variables? This question goes beyond the
internal considerations for adequate study controls
and is therefore a matter of _____ validity.

■ external

3 The concern of external validity is essentially that of *generalization*. By generalization we refer to the extrapolation of treatment effects or effects of the _____ variable to other populations or conditions.

■ independent

4 Extrapolation beyond the study samples and conditions is hazardous. Such generalization requires considerable faith in the process of _____ (deductive/inductive) inference.

■ inductive

5 One factor that may affect the generalizability of research findings is the difference between the study samples and the population to which the study may be _____ .

■ generalized

6 If the selection of subjects for the study samples is biased, generalization from the study samples to a larger _____ would be risky.

■ population

7 For example, it was found that subjects selected from a school enrolling children of middle-income parents evidenced greater achievement under conditions of flexible scheduling than under fixed scheduling. It _____(would/would not) be safe to assume such a finding would hold for children of low-income parents.

■
■ would not

8 In effect, the nonrepresentativeness of the children selected in frame 7 (which may not jeopardize internal validity) raises serious questions of generalizability to children of low-income parents and thus could threaten the _____ validity of the study.

■
■ external

9 This is so because there may be particular psychological characteristics of the study children or predisposing factors in the schools of middle-income students that would enhance their responsiveness to flexible scheduling. Thus, the concern here is with the *interaction* of selection and _____ effects.

■
■ treatment

10 In addition, prior experience of the study subjects to innovative school procedures may create a positive responsiveness to "new" structural arrangements. Were this the case for the study children in frame 7, generalization to all children of middle-income parents _____(would/would not) be problematic.

■
■ would

11 The greater the subject selection bias the more like-
    ly is the interaction of selection and treatment to
    occur and, thus, to affect the _____ _____
    of a study.

■
■   external validity

12 It must be pointed out that differences on some vari-
    able(s) between study samples and a larger popula-
    tion does not, of itself, produce a selection by
    treatment interaction. The crucial consideration is
    whether the differences between the study samples
    and the larger population _____ with the inde-
    pendent variable.

■
■   interact

13 Another factor that may affect the external validity
    of a study is what has been termed *pretest sensiti-
    zation*. As the term implies, such sensitization
    would produce a _____ by treatment interaction.

■
■   testing

14 If the responses to the pretest affect the responses
    of the study subjects to the treatment, then this
    testing by treatment interaction would affect the
    _____ _____ of the study.

■
■   external validity

15 The results of a study in which there was an inter-
    action of testing and treatment could not be
    _____ to similar populations.

■
■   generalized

16   The effects of pretesting on the responses to treat-
     ments are most likely to occur for attitude, opinion,
     and personality measures. Thus, pretest sensiti-
     zation is likely to be _____(less/greater) for a
     questionnaire on racial affiliation than for a test
     requiring the application of scientific principles.

■   greater

STUDY 13-1

A study was conducted to determine whether a randomly assigned classroom seating arrangement
would increase cross-racial contacts. This seating arrangement was to be compared with the
"usual" student-selected seating pattern. A
sociometric choice criterion measure was administered before and after treatment. The researcher hoped to be in a position to recommend
a basis for student seating at the time a racial
integration plan was put into effect for the
forthcoming school year.
   The group that was randomly assigned to seats
showed a significantly greater increase in cross-
racial choice during the school year.

---

17   The treatment in Study 13-1 was the _____
     _____(student selected/randomly assigned) seat-
     ing arrangement.

■   randomly assigned

18   It is reasonable to suspect that the response to the
     treatment was, in part, a result of the administra-
     tion of the sociometric _____(pretest/posttest).

■   pretest

19 The facilitating effects on racial affiliation through seating arrangement cannot be meaningfully determined because the treatment effect is confounded by _____ .

■ testing/pretesting

20 Pretesting on sociometric choice would not be a usual procedure before assigning classroom seating. Therefore, the results of Study 13-1 cannot be _____ to non-pretested populations.

■ generalized

21 Were an unobtrusive data-gathering technique used to ascertain cross-racial contacts there likely _____ (would/would not) be a testing by treatment interaction effect.

■ would not

22 A testing by treatment interaction can occur for the posttest as well as for the _____ .

■ pretest

23 It is conceivable that the posttest may provide an additional opportunity for the treatment effects to take hold. The effect would be greatest where the _____ was visibly related to the treatment.

■ posttest

24 The research described in Study 13-1 _____(does/ does not) have a strong possibility for posttest treatment interaction.

■■ does

25 In the school setting described in Study 13-1, the random assignment of seats is so out of the ordinary it is likely that experimental subjects would figure out the purpose of the study from the _____ .

■■ posttest

26 Even if no pretest were given, sociometric choice, as observed unobtrusively, might yield results for the treatment condition different from that where a questionnaire was administered as a _____ .

■■ posttest

27 Knowledge of participating in a study may produce changes in the subjects' responses. This factor, like the previously mentioned factors, will affect the _____ _____ of a study.

■■ external validity

28 The term for this effect is the *reactive effect* of treatments. Teachers' knowledge of the purpose of a study will likely _____(increase/decrease) the reactive effect.

■■ increase

29 Not informing subjects of the purpose of a study
    will make _____ (less/more) probable the reactive
    effect of treatments.

■ less

30 Students in schools in which experimentation is a
    usual pattern are likely to show _____ (less/more)
    reactive effect to curriculum innovation than would
    be the case for students attending a highly struc-
    tured school program.

■ less

31 Reactive effects may not always be "positive" in the
    sense that knowledge will increase the efficacy of
    the treatment. For example, the knowledge of being
    a study participant may lead to caution, anxiety, or
    self-censuring behavior. Similar nonexperimental
    conditions may not produce such _____ effects.

■ reactive

32 In medicine, a placebo (nonefficacious treatment) is
    sometimes used to study the effects of medication so
    as to control for _____ _____ .

■ reactive effects

33 Because a patient does not know he is given a place-
    bo, he is likely to believe the "medication" will be
    effective. Therefore, reactive effects are likely
    to be _____ (similar/different) for both the
    medication and placebo groups.

■ similar

34 Minimizing the obtrusiveness of a treatment will re-
    duce reactive effects and increase the repre-
    sentativeness of the treatment effect. Thus the gen-
    eralization to other environmental conditions will be
    be _____ (increased/decreased).

■ increased

35 *Multiple treatment interference* occurs when two or
    more _____ are administered simultaneously or
    consecutively to the same subjects.

■ treatments

STUDY 13-2

In a study designed to improve the achievement
of economically disadvantaged students approxi-
mately 15 changes in the usual school program
were instituted. Only one comparison group was
used. The results indicated significant changes
favoring the experimental program. An analysis
of the cost of the study revealed that it was
impossible to institute the experimental program
beyond its present scope. The school board re-
quested that the two or three features of the
experimental program which seemed most effective
be selected from among the 15 changes. These
selected features would then be analyzed for
cost and instituted if feasible.

---

36 Study 13-2 has been so designed as to make it
    _____ (possible/impossible) to separate out
    the individual treatment effects.

■ impossible

37 It may be that one of the elements of the experimental program produced the improvement in achievement or all 15 elements contributed to the change. In Study 13-2 treatment effects are confounded, thus effecting the _____ _____ of the study.

■
■ external validity

38 The experimental program in Study 13-2 undoubtedly could not be replicated in fact. Thus, such a study would not be _____ to other environmental conditions

■
■ generalizable

39 Treatments may be administered consecutively or alternately with repeated measurements taken on the dependent variable. The problem with regard to multiple treatment interference in this instance is that the effect of one treatment _____(can/cannot) be eliminated when examining the effects of other treatments.

■
■ cannot

40 The term "interference" implies nonindependence of _____ effects.

■
■ treatment

41 Treatments that have independent effects _____ (will/will not) show multiple treatment interference.

■
■ will not

VI.

RESEARCH DESIGNS

In part 5 we discussed various factors that can threaten the internal and external validity of a research study. Our desire, of course, is to conduct our research project in such a way as to eliminate, or at least minimize, as many of these threats as possible

There are many ways that we can conduct a given research project. One of the tasks of the researcher is to choose a plan that will enhance the validity of the study. The various plans from which the researcher must choose are called research designs.

In Sets 14, 15, and 16 we will present a number of research designs. These sets will present three types of designs--preexperimental, experimental, and ·quasi-experimental-- and will distinguish among them in terms of how well the threats to internal and extrenal validity are controlled. A symbol system will be introduced for depicting the various designs.

14.

PREEXPERIMENTAL RESEARCH DESIGNS

1 It is always the desire of the experimenter to eliminate, or at least reduce, any threats to the internal and external _____ of a study.

■ validity

2 For research results to be generalizable, they must
first be obtained through properly conducted experiments. That is, to have high external validity a
study must first have high _____ validity.

■ internal

3 A study that has high internal validity may have
_____ (only low/only high/either
low or high) external validity.

■ either low or high

4   The experimenter should always choose a research design that enhances both the _____ and _____ _____ of the study.

■ internal, external validity

5   In this and the next two sets we will examine various research designs and determine the extent to which they reduce or eliminate threats to validity. This set provides some procedures that are termed "preexperimental designs." As the name implies, these _____(are/are not) true experimental designs.

■ are not

6   We shall use symbols to depict the components of the various designs. The symbol X shall represent the "treatment" that is employed in the study. Thus, X will represent the _____(dependent/independent) variable in the study.

■ independent

7   We shall use the symbol O to represent measurements obtained on individuals in the study. Thus, O will represent measurements on the _____ variable.

■ dependent

8 It is customary to depict the order of events by
   writing the symbols in sequence from left to right.
   Our first preexperimental design is:

DESIGN NO. 1 (Preexperimental)

One-Group Posttest Design

$X \qquad O$

X: Treatment (Independent Variable)

O: Posttest (Dependent Variable)

Design No. 1 indicates that we obtain a measure on
the dependent variable _____(before/after) the
introduction of the treatment.

■ after

9 Design No. 1 is called the "One-Group Posttest
   Design" because measurements are obtained on
   _____(only/more than) one sample at _____
   (only/more than) one time point.

■ only, only

10 A measurement taken before treatment is called the
    _____(pre/post) test. A measurement taken after
    treatment is called the _____(pre/post) test.

■ pre, post

11 In Design No. 1 there is only a _____ (pretest/
    posttest).

■ posttest

STUDY 14-1 *Example of a One-Group Posttest Study*

A group of third grade students were given
instruction in the difference between toads and
frogs. They were then administered a test to
determine if they know the difference between
these two animals.

---

12 From Study 14-1 it would be _____ (possible/
    impossible) to ascertain whether or not the students
    know the difference between toads and frogs.

■ possible

13 It would be _____ (possible/impossible) to
    determine whether the students' knowledge was the re-
    sult of the instruction.

■ impossible

14 We _____ (do/do not) have a measure of the stu-
    dents' knowledge of toads and frogs before the in-
    struction was given.

■ do not

15 To determine if there was any gain in knowledge dur-
    ing the instructional period, we need both a _____
    test and a _____ test.

■   pre, post

16 In the One-Group Posttest Design, we _____(can/
    cannot) say that the measurements we obtain on the
    dependent variable (*O*) result from the effects of
    the independent variable (*X*).

■   cannot

17 This is true because we have no measure of the de-
    pendent variable _____(before/after) the intro-
    duction of the treatment.

■   before

18 The second type of preexperimental design is:

Design No. 2 (Preexperimental)

One Group Pretest-Posttest Design

$$O_1 \; X \; O_2$$

X: Treatment

O_1: Pretest

O_2: Posttest

Design No. 2 requires _____(one/two) measurement(s) of the dependent variable.

■ two

19 Design No. 2 calls for a _____ test, followed by the _____ , followed by a _____ test.

■ pre, treatment, post

STUDY 14-2 Example of a One-Group Pretest-Posttest Study

A ninth grade teacher was concerned with assessing how much knowledge the students in his chemistry class acquired as a result of his instruction. He gave them the same chemistry test at the beginning and at the end of the semester and noted that their scores improved.

---

20 In Study 14-2 there is a _____ test and a _____ test of knowledge of chemistry.

■ pre, post

21 It _____ (is/is not) possible that events other than the instruction in the chemistry class resulted in the improvement in the scores on the test.

■ is

22 If, during the semester, dramatic events in chemistry were taking place, it is possible that the students' increase in knowledge resulted from exposure to the news media rather than to class _____ .

■ instruction

23 In Study 14-2 the effects of history _____ (may/cannot) account for changes from O_1 to O_2. Thus, this is one threat to the _____ validity of this study.

■ may, internal

24 In the One-Group Pretest-Posttest Design we have noted that the effects of _____ are not controlled.

■ history

25 Recall that maturation can also be a threat to the internal validity of a study. It _____(is/is not) possible for the students to show an increase in knowledge solely because of maturation.

■
■ is

26 In Design No. 2 it is possible that the taking of the pretest may affect the results of the _____.

■
■ posttest

27 In Study 14-2 any increase in knowledge of chemistry could have been caused by the taking of the _____. This is called the "_____" effect.

■
■ pretest, testing

28 In Design No. 2 we may say that the testing effect is _____(controlled/uncontrolled).

■
■ uncontrolled

29 Up to this point, we have specified three threats to the internal validity of studies using the One-Group Pretest-Posttest Design. In such studies we have noted that changes from pretest to posttest may result from _____ , _____ , or the _____ effect.

■
■ history, maturation, testing

30 If the students had been purposefully selected because of their extremely low pretest scores, then
the increase in scores from pretest to posttest
could result from _____ regression and not
from the _____ variable.

■ statistical, independent

31 Thus, in the One-Group Pretest-Posttest Design the
changes between O_1 and O_2 may result from statistical _____ . This possibility results in a
serious threat to the _____ validity of studies
where extreme groups are used.

■ regression, internal

32 If the manner in which the chemistry test was administered differed from pretest to posttest, this
could have caused differences in the level of the
scores. This is known as the _____
threat to internal validity.

■ instrumentation

33 In the One-Group Pretest-Posttest Design, unless the
pretests and posttests are the same and their admin-
istrations are identical, there is an
_____ threat to the validity of such studies.

■ instrumentation

34 We have seen that there are many threats to the
_____ validity of this design.

■ internal

35 Because of these threats, experimenters using the
One-Group Pretest-Posttest Design _____ (can/
cannot) determine the degree to which changes occurring from pretest to posttest are the result of the
_____ variable.

■ cannot, independent

36 The third type of preexperimental design is:

DESIGN NO. 3 (Preexperimental)

Intact-Group Posttest Design

$$X \qquad\qquad O_2$$

$$O_4$$

X: Treatment

O_2 and O_4: Posttests

Design No. 3 requires that there be ____ (one/two)
group(s) in the study.

■ two

37 Design No. 3 indicates that the treatment is administered to _____ (one/both) group(s).

■ one

38 In Design No. 3 pretests on the dependent variable are given to _____ (one/both/neither) group(s); posttests are given to _____ (one/both/neither) group(s).

■ neither, both

39 In Design No. 3 the dashed line separating the two groups indicates that they are "intact" groups. This means that the individuals _____ (have/ have not) been randomly assigned to the two groups.

■ have not

STUDY 14-3   Example of an Intact-Group Posttest Study

A principal wished to assess the value of having guest speakers participate in high school civics classes. He arranged for a series of guests to speak to Mr. Adam's civics class while Mrs. Baker's class was conducted without guest speakers. At the end of the semester the principal found that Mr. Adam's class scored higher than Mrs. Baker's class on the final civics exam.

---

40 Study 14-3 is an example of an Intact-Group Posttest Design because the students have not been _____ assigned to Mr. Adam's and Mrs. Baker's classes.

■ randomly

41 It _____(is/is not) possible that Mr. Adam's class began the semester with a greater knowledge of civics than Mrs. Baker's class.

■
■ is

42 The difference between the posttest scores for the two classes may result from their initial differences in knowledge of civics rather than the _____ variable.

■
■ independent

43 There may be a bias in the selection procedure used for assigning students to the two classes that resulted in the brighter students being placed in Mr. Adam's class. This would cause a _____ threat to the internal validity of the study.

■
■ selection

44 It is impossible to tell the extent to which the guest speakers caused a difference between the two classes on the _____ variable.

■
■ dependent

45 Assuming that both classes had similar experiences outside class, we may say that the threat of _____ effects to the internal validity of the study has been controlled.

■
■ history

46 In the Intact-Group Posttest Design, "testing"
    _____ (is/is not) a threat to internal validity
    because a _____ is not given to either group.

■ is not, pretest

47 If the same posttests are administered to both
    groups in the same fashion, there would be no threat
    to internal validity from _____ .

■ instrumentation

48 In the Intact-Group Posttest Design, statistical re-
    gression would not be a threat to internal validity
    because no _____ was given to either group.

■ pretest

49 In Study 14-3, if the two classes were comparable
    initially, but a large number of Mrs. Baker's
    brighter students transferred from her class during
    the semester, this _____ (may/may not) have re-
    sulted in a difference between the two classes on
    the posttests. This is called a _____ threat
    to internal validity.

■ may, mortality

50 A characteristic of all preexperimental designs is
    the inability of the experimenter to control various
    _____ to the _____ validity of the study.

■ threats, internal

51 Because of uncontrolled threats to validity, it is impossible for the experimenter to determine the extent to which measurements on the _____ variable result from the _____ variable.

■ dependent, independent

52 For a study to be valuable, we must be able to control _____ to internal validity so that differences in measurements on the dependent variable result from the _____ .

■ threats, treatment

183:

SET

15.

EXPERIMENTAL DESIGNS

1 In contrast to the preexperimental designs presented in Set 14, in which a number of sources of invalidity were not controlled, this set will present three true experimental designs. They are called experimental designs because they provide methods for _____ threats to validity.

▪ controlling

2   The first experimental design that we shall discuss is:

DESIGN NO. 4 (Experimental)

        Pretest-Posttest Control Group Design

$$R \quad O_1 \quad X \quad O_2$$

$$R \quad O_3 \qquad O_4$$

X: Treatment

O_1 and O_3: Pretests

O_2 and O_4: Posttests

R: Random Assignment

Design No. 4 indicates that there are two comparison groups. The experimental group receives the treatment (X) and the control group does not. Both groups _____ (do/do not) receive a pretest and a posttest.

■ do

3   In Design No. 4, the letter R preceding both pretests indicates that the individuals in the study have been _____ assigned to the two groups.

■ randomly

185:

4   Design No. 4 _____(does/does not) control for
    selection bias as a threat to the internal validity
    of the study, because individuals are assigned
    _____ to the two groups.

■   does, randomly

STUDY 15-1   *Example of a Pretest-Posttest Control*
             Group Study

The manager of a manufacturing firm wanted to
determine if providing employees with free snacks
during the working day would improve their production rates. A randomly selected group of 50
employees were used in this experiment; 25 were
randomly assigned to the "free snack" group and
25 were not provided snacks. He measured the
production rates of the two groups before intro-
ducing the snack program. After a three-month
period he again measured their production rates
and found that the "free snack" group showed
greater improvement in their production rates
than did the other group.

---

5   In Study 15-1 the manager could be fairly certain
    that the two groups in the study were quite
    _____ (similar/different) in their motivation
    to do a good job before the study.

■   similar

6   Also, because of random assignment, both groups will
    probably be _____ (similar/different) in their
    absentee rates during the period of the project.

■   similar

7 The composition of the two groups in Study 15-1
_____ (will/will not) differ greatly on sex, educational level, age, etc.

■ will not

8 In fact, because of the random assignment process,
it can be assumed that both groups are initially
quite comparable on _____ (few/all) variables.

■ all

9 Therefore, because of randomization, there is no
threat to internal validity from _____ .

■ selection

10 Because the time period between the pretest and the
posttest is the same for both the "free snack" and
the "no snack" groups, the amount of change in production rate over time due to maturation should be
_____ (the same/different) for both groups.

■ the same

11 Thus far we have seen that the Pretest-Posttest Control Group Design controls for threats to internal
validity from _____ and _____ .

■ selection, maturation

12　In Study 15-1, because of random assignment we would expect that the "history" of both groups during the experimental period would be _____ (the same/different).

■　the same

13　Therefore, we can assume that history as a threat to internal validity _____ (is/is not) controlled in the Pretest-Posttest Control Group Design.

■　is

14　Because neither group was selected on the basis of either initial high or low production rates, statistical _____ would not pose a threat to the internal validity of the study.

■　regression

15　The four threats to internal validity that we may assume are controlled when an experimenter uses the Pretest-Posttest Control Group Design are _____ , _____ , _____ , and _____ _____ .

■　selection, maturation, history, statistical regression

16　If the manager of the manufacturing firm sets up an elaborate testing program to determine the initial production rates of both groups, the administration of the pretest _____ (may/will not) affect the production rates of both groups on posttest.

■　may

17 Thus, one threat to the internal validity of studies
    using Design No. 4 that is uncontrolled is the
    _____ effect.

■ testing

18 Where an experimenter is relatively certain that the
    administration of a pretest will have negligible ef-
    fect on the posttest, Design No. 4 is desirable be-
    cause it provides a measurement of the initial
    comparability of both groups on the _____ vari-
    able.

■ dependent

19 Even if Design No. 4 provides control for many
    threats to internal validity, a threat to the exter-
    nal validity may be present because of _____
    (pretest/posttest) sensitization.

■ pretest

20 In Study 15-1, if the pretest that the manager uses
    to determine initial production rates alerts the
    employees that they are involved in an experiment,
    this knowledge may cause them to work harder to im-
    prove their _____ _____ than they normally
    would.

■ production rates

189:

21 After taking the pretest, the employees in both
    groups may be more motivated to do good work and
    will therefore no longer be _____ of all
    the employees in the factory. This will result in a
    threat to the _____ validity of the study.

■ representative, external

22 Another type of experimental design is:

┌───┐
│   │
│   DESIGN NO. 5   (Experimental)   │
│   │
│   Posttest Only Control Group Design   │
│   │
│   R X O_2 │
│   │
│   R O_4 │
│   │
│   X: Treatment   │
│   │
│ O_2 and O_4: Posttest   │
│   │
│   R: Random assignment   │
│   │
└───┘

    Design No. 5 indicates that the individuals in both
    groups have been _____ selected.

■ randomly

23 In Design No. 5, the threats to internal validity
    from selection, maturation, history, and regression
    _____ (have/have not) been controlled.

■ have

24 The reason that so many threats to internal validity
    are controlled in Design No. 5 is that the individ-
    uals in the study are _____ assigned to the two
    groups.

■
■   randomly

STUDY 15-2 *Example of a Posttest Only Control*
            Group Study

A school psychologist wished to test the hypothesis that student attitudes toward education would
be improved if students attended a series of
audio-visual presentations on the value of obtaining an education. To test this hypothesis,
he randomly selected 200 students from the student
body and randomly assigned 100 of them to attend
a series of audio-visual presentations throughout the school year. The other sample of 100
students did not attend the presentations. At
the end of the school year he administered an
"education attitude scale" to both groups and
found more positive attitudes in the group that
attended the audio-visual presentations.

---

25 In Study 15-2 assigning students randomly to the two
    groups would lead the school psychologist to con-
    clude that many threats to internal validity are
    _____ .

■
■   controlled

26 In addition, any threats to external validity from
    _____ sensitization are not present in this
    design.

■
■   pretest

27 The school psychologist probably did not choose to obtain initial ratings using the "education attitude scale" because he feared that it might _____ students to the nature of the experiment.

■ sensitize

28 On the other hand, without a pretest, the school psychologist does not have any information on the attitudes the students held regarding the value of education before the experiment began. He assumes they held comparable attitudes because of their _____ assignment to the two groups.

■ random

29 Whenever a researcher suspects that there is a serious threat to the external validity of a study from pretest sensitization, it would be wise to choose Design No. ___(4/5).

■ 5

30 The drawback to Design No. 5 is that, regardless of the assumption that the groups are comparable because of randomization, the researcher does not *know* exactly the status of the groups on the _____ variable before the experiment.

■ dependent

31 However, where there is a clear threat to external validity from pretesting, Design No. ___(4/5) is preferable to Design No. ___(4/5) particularly if there are _____(small/large) samples in the study.

■ 5, 4, large

32 A more complex type of experimental design is:

DESIGN NO. 6 (Experimental)

Solomon Four-Group Design

Group A R O_1 X O_2

Group B R O_3 O_4

Group C R X O_6

Group D R O_8

X: Treatment

O_1 and O_3: Pretests

O_2, O_4, O_6, and O_8: Posttests

R: Random Assignment

Design No. 6 incorporates the features of Design No. ____ and Design No. ____ .

∎ 4, 5

33 In Design No. 6 there is(are) ____ (one/two) experimental group(s) and ____ (one/two) control group(s).

∎ two, two

34 In Design No. 6 a pretest is given to ____ (one/two) experimental group(s) and to ____ (one/two) control group(s).

∎ one, one

STUDY 15-3 *Example of a Solomon Four-Group Study*

An educational researcher wished to test the hypothesis that the commonly held stereotypes toward handicapped students could be reduced if students had opportunity to be involved in group activities with handicapped students. He randomly selected 200 students and then randomly assigned 50 of them to each of four samples. Samples A and C were scheduled to participate in a series of activities with handicapped students, Samples B and D did not have these experiences. All four groups were administered an attitude questionnaire at the end of the school year. However, only Groups A and B were administered this questionnaire at the beginning of the school year.

35 In Study 15-3 the Solomon Four-Group Design permits the researcher to infer that the four groups are comparable on all variables because the 200 students were _____ assigned to the four groups.

■
■ randomly

36 It is possible to assess the amount of change in attitude that might be attributable to history or maturational effects by examining the pretest and posttest attitude ratings of Group ___(A/B/C/D).

■
■ B

37 It would then be possible to assess the differential change in attitudes that may be attributable to the group activities (X) by comparing the pretest and posttest ratings of Groups ___ and ___ .

■
■ A, B

38 Also, the Solomon Four-Group Design permits the re-searcher to determine if the administration of the pretest attitude questionnaire had any effect on how the students responded to the _____ attitude questionnaire.

■ posttest

39 This effect can be determined in two ways: by com-paring the posttest ratings of Groups ___ and ___ , and by comparing the posttest ratings of Groups ___ and ___ .

■ A, C, B, D

40 Thus, the Solomon Four-Group Design controls for all threats to internal validity and, because Groups C and D are not pretested, it is possible to assess the degree to which _____ validity is threat-ened by _____ sensitization.

■ external, pretest

41 One feature that distinguishes all experimental de-signs from the preexperimental designs is that exper-imental designs always include at least one _____ group.

■ control

42 A second feature is that in all experimental designs the individuals are _____ assigned to experimen-tal and control groups.

■ randomly

43 This process of random assignment to groups is most
    important in research because it permits the re-
    searcher to infer that the groups are initially
    _____(comparable/different) on all variables,
    including the dependent variable.

■ comparable

16:

QUASI-EXPERIMENTAL DESIGNS

1 In Set 14 we discussed various preexperimental designs in which few if any threats to internal validity were controlled. Quasi-experimental designs control for some but not all threats to validity and
therefore are _____(more/less) preferable than preexperimental designs.

■ more

2 In cases where random assignment to groups is not
possible, we cannot use _____ designs.

■ experimental

3 In such cases, it may be possible to use a quasi-experimental design. The first quasi-experimental design we shall present is:

DESIGN NO. 7 (Quasi-Experimental)

Nonequivalent Control Group Design

$$O_1 \quad X \quad O_2$$
- - - - - - - - - - -
$$O_3 \qquad O_4$$

X: Treatment

O_1 and O_3: Pretests

O_2 and O_4: Posttests

Design No. 7 differs from Design No. 4 (page 185) in that the groups in Design No. 7 are _____(intact/random). For this reason, Design No. 7 is _____ (superior/inferior) to Design No. 4.

■ intact, inferior

4 Design No. 7 is _____(superior/inferior) to Design No. 2 because of the inclusion of a _____ _____.

■ superior, control group

5   Design No. 7 is _____ (superior/inferior) to
    Design No. 3 (page 179) because it incorporates a
    _____ of the dependent variable.

■   superior, pretest

STUDY 16-1   Example of a Nonequivalent Control
             Group Study

An instructor of educational research courses
wondered if the assignment of programmed instruction materials would result in her students
showing a greater gain in knowledge of research
methods than when programmed instruction materials were not assigned. She taught her Tuesday
and Wednesday classes in the same way but assigned
programmed instruction material to the Tuesday
class only. She gave both classes a pretest and
a posttest on a research methods knowledge test
and obtained the results graphed below.

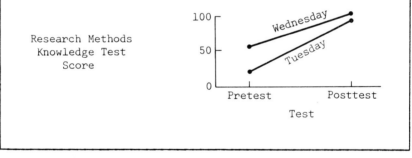

Research Methods
Knowledge Test
Score

6   In Study 16-1 the selection of students for the two
    classes was _____ (controlled/uncontrolled).

■   uncontrolled

7   Therefore, the internal validity of Study 16-1 may be threatened because of _____ effects.

■■ selection

8   We can determine the degree to which a selection factor resulted in a difference between the two groups by comparing their scores on the _____ of the dependent variable.

■■ pretest

9   The results in Study 16-1 indicate that the Wednesday class has _____ (lower/higher) pretest scores than the Tuesday class.

■■ higher

10   This indicates that there _____ (was/was not) a difference between the two classes because of _____ effects.

■■ was, selection

11   It _____ (is/is not) possible to determine if the two classes differed on other variables that may affect the dependent variable, such as experience or motivation.

■■ is not

12 The results indicate that there was a _____
    (lesser/greater) gain in the Tuesday class, although
    they scored _____(lower/higher) on the pretest.

■ greater, lower

13 This might lead the instructor to suspect that the
    Tuesday class was an extremely low-scoring group and
    that their gain might result from statistical
    _____ .

■ regression

14 On the other hand, if both groups had similar levels
    of scores on the pretest, it could be assumed that
    if statistical regression were a factor, it would af-
    fect both groups _____(differently/similarly).

■ similarly

15 If the out-of-class experiences of the two groups
    were not markedly different during the experimental
    period, the instructor could consider that _____
    effects were not a serious threat to the internal
    validity of the study.

■ history

16 Also, since the period between pretests and post-
    tests was the same for both classes, there was proba-
    bly no differential effect on the dependent variable
    because of _____ .

■ maturation

17   Since both classes had a pretest and a posttest, the threat from _____ is controlled.

■ testing

18   Because the Nonequivalent Control Group Design uses intact groups, we are unable to determine the extent to which they differ on variables that might affect the _____(pre/post)-test scores on the _____ variable.

■ post, dependent

19   Therefore, the major threat to the internal validity of a study using the Nonequivalent Control Group Design is the _____ factor.

■ selection

20 Another quasi-experimental design that is sometimes used when it is not possible to employ an experimental design is:

DESIGN NO. 8   (Quasi-Experimental)

Time Series Design

$$O_1 \; O_2 \; O_3 \; O_4 \; X \; O_5 \; O_6 \; O_7 \; O_8$$

X: Treatment

O: Measurements on the Dependent Variable

In Design No. 8 there are a series of measurements on the _____ variable preceding the _____ and a series of measurements following the _____.

■ dependent, treatment, treatment

21 Design No. 8 indicates that all measurements are obtained from _____ (the same/different) group(s).

■ the same

22 The Time Series Design is one in which a _____ is introduced during a series of measurements on the _____ variable.

■ treatment, dependent

STUDY 16-2 Example of a Time Series Study

An experimental psychologist developed a drug designed to increase the reaction time of rats
when subjected to electric shock.   To test his
drug he recorded the reaction times of a group of
rats on each of four trials.   He then administered
the drug and recorded the reaction times on four
more trials.   The time intervals between the
trials were equal.   The average reaction times are
reported below.

Trial	Average Reaction Time (in seconds)
O_1	.20
O_2	.18
O_3	.17
O_4	.15
X (Treatment)	
O_5	.05
O_6	.07
O_7	.06
O_8	.08

23 In Study 16-2, measurements at O_1, O_2, O_3, and O_4
indicate that the reaction times of the rats are
gradually getting _____(faster/slower) over time.

■ faster

24 From O_4 to O_5 there is a _____(minimal/
considerable) acceleration in reaction time.

■ considerable

25 This sharp acceleration in reaction time occurred immediately after the administration of the _____ .

■ drug

26 The measurements from O_5 to O_8 indicate that the reaction times are slowly _____ (accelerating/decelerating).

■ decelerating

27 The measurements clearly indicate that all of the pretest reaction times (O_1 through O_4) are _____ (slower/faster) than the posttest reaction times (O_5 through O_8).

■ slower

28 Because the trials were equally spaced, it is _____ (likely/unlikely) that history threatens the internal validity of the study.

■ unlikely

29 For there to be a history effect invalidating the study, an extraneous historical event would have had to occur simultaneously with the _____ variable.

■ independent

30 The effects of maturation, testing, and instrumenta-
    tion could be affecting the reaction time. It
    _____(is/is not) likely that they account for the
    unusual change in reaction time that occurred be-
    tween O_4 and O_5.

■ is not

31 The value of the Time Series Design is that, in the
    absence of a plausible alternative explanation, a
    sharp change in the trend of measurements on the de-
    pendent variable immediately following the treatment
    is usually attributable to the effects of the
    _____.

■ treatment

32 A third quasi-experimental design is:

DESIGN NO. 9 (Quasi-Experimental)

Equivalent Time Series Design

$$X_1 \ O_1 \ X_0 \ O_2 \ X_1 \ O_3 \ X_0 \ O_4$$

X_1: One Treatment

X_0: Another Treatment

O: Measurements on Dependent Variable

Studies using Design No. 9 require _____
(one/more than one) experimental group(s).

■ one

33 Design No. 9 indicates that there are two _____,
    which are alternatively administered to the sample.

■ treatments

34 In Design No. 9 each administration of a treatment is
    followed by a measurement on the _____ variable.

■ dependent

---

*STUDY 16-3   Example of an Equivalent Time Series
              Study*

In the past Mr. Clark has always shown a series
of movies to his history classes. He decided to
see if the students' attitudes regarding the
study of history could be improved if he took
them on field trips to historical sites. He
structured his curriculum so that every other
week his class viewed movies and on the alternate
weeks they visited historical sites. Each Friday
he administered a rating scale on which the class
indicated their feelings toward the study of history. The results of the first six weeks are
graphed below.

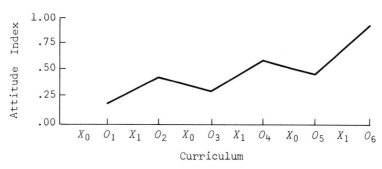

X_0: Movies

X_1: Visitations

O: Weekly Attitude Ratings

---

35 The design used in Study 16-3 is called quasi-
    experimental because there is no _____ group.

■ control

36 The results indicate that there is an overall trend
    over time toward _____ (negative/positive) atti-
    tudinal change.

■ positive

37 There is always a decrease in attitude following
    _____ and an increase following _____ _____ .

■ movies, field trips

38 The data produced by the Equivalent Time Series De-
    sign used in Study 16-3 reveals that attitudes are
    higher on weeks in which there are _____ _____
    and lower on weeks in which there are _____ .

■ field trips, movies

39 As with the Time Series Design (Design No. 8), the
    Equivalent Time Series Design is of value if it can
    be continued for a number of trials because it can
    detect _____ in the measurements.

■ trends

208:

40 Because of the alternating treatments, the Equivalent Time Series Design is most appropriate where
the effect of each treatment is _____(permanent/
temporary).

■ temporary

41 Because of the many alternations of treatments, there
may be a threat to the external validity of such studies from multiple _____ interference.

■ treatment

42 When using Design No. 9, to avoid a pattern of responses from developing because of the regularity of
treatment alternation, the treatments could be presented in _____ order.

■ random

43 The strength of most quasi-experimental designs lies
in their ability to detect _____ in multiple measurements on the dependent variable.

■ trends

44 There are many quasi-experimental designs. None of
them are as satisfactory as experimental designs because they lack control of some of the threats to
_____ and _____ validity.

■ internal, external

45 Yet where experimental designs are not possible,
there may be value in employing a _____-experimental
design, rather than a _____ design.

■
■ quasi, preexperimental

VII.

MODELS FOR STRUCTURING RESEARCH

The researcher should design the research project to
be as efficient as possible yet yield maximal information. The design that the researcher adopts will
permit him to structure the data organization and
analysis in a way that will provide answers to a number of research questions simultaneously. The various models for structuring research in the behavioral
sciences are presented in Sets 17, 18, and 19. The
"Two-Group Simple Randomized" and "Random Replications"
models are presented in Set 17. The importance of
random selection and random assignment are stressed.
Sets 18 and 19 introduce simple and complex factorial modes, respectively. The use of such models for
the study of the simultaneous effect of more than
one independent variable on the dependent variable
is discussed. A discussion is presented of the main
effects of manipulated and nonmanipulated independent
variables and the interaction among them. A number
of examples are offered to illustrate the use of
each model.

17:

TWO-GROUP SIMPLE RANDOMIZED AND RANDOM REPLICATIONS
MODELS

1 In Set 15 we examined three experimental designs.
   There are various *models* for structuring the samples
   within each of these designs. The correct model we
   choose in a particular study depends upon the number
   of _____ variables to be studied and the number of _____ variables to be controlled.

■
■ independent, extraneous

2 We learned in Set 15 that one of the basic requirements for experimental designs is that there be at
   least _____(one/two) sample(s) involved in the study.

■
■ two

3 Also, for a design to be experimental, the members
   assigned to the various samples must be _____
   selected.

■
■ randomly

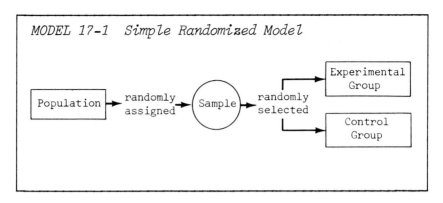

MODEL 17-1   *Simple Randomized Model*

Population → randomly assigned → Sample → randomly selected → Experimental Group / Control Group

4 Model 17-1 presents the Simple Randomized Model for sample selection. It is appropriate for use with both the Pretest-Posttest Control Group Design and the _____ _____ Control Group Design.

■ Posttest Only

5 Model 17-1 can be extended for use in the Solomon Four-Group Design through the random selection of _____ samples.

■ four

6 The first step in obtaining samples for the Simple Randomized Model is to define the _____ .

■ population

7 When the characteristics of the population have been defined, it is then necessary to _____ select a sample.

■ randomly

8   Using Model 17-1 for sample selection is likely to
    lead to a sample that is _____ of the
    population, and, therefore, contributes to the
    _____ (internal/external) validity of the study.

■ representative, external

9   A further requirement of this model is that individ-
    uals, after being randomly selected from the popula-
    tion, be randomly assigned to the _____ and
    _____ groups.

■ experimental, control

10 The Simple Randomized Model yields two groups repre-
    sentative of the _____ from which they were
    drawn.

■ population

> STUDY 17-1   *Example of a Study Using the Simple*
>   *Randomized Model with the Pretest-*
>   *Posttest Control Group Design*
>
> We wish to compare two groups of students who
> have been randomly selected and randomly assigned.
> One group received the usual math program and the
> other group received the SMSG math program. We
> hypothesize greater gains for the SMSG group. To
> determine which group gained most in mathematical
> concepts during the year, we test each group be-
> fore the program begins and after the program
> ends. We then compare the amount of gain for the
> two groups over this one year period.

11 It is reasonable to assume the groups were initially
    comparable on mathematical concepts because they
    were selected using the Simple _____ Model.

■■ Randomized

12 Further, it is assumed that the randomly assigned
    groups are comparable on all _____ variables
    that are correlated with the dependent variable.

■■ extraneous

13 In this study, the independent variable _____
    (was/was not) manipulated.

■■ was

14 This study is of the _____(experimental/
    nonexperimental) hypothesis-testing type.

■■ experimental

15 The model used in this study is referred to as Sim-
    ple Randomized Model because students were randomly
    selected and _____(were/were not) stratified on
    control variables.

■■ were not

16 In the Simple Randomized Model the students have
been both randomly drawn from the same population
and _____ assigned to the experimental and control groups.

∎ randomly

17 In summary, we can describe Study 17-1 as
_____ hypothesis-testing research employing
a _____ - _____ Group Design in which samples
have been selected using the _____ _____
_____ Model.

∎ experimental, Pretest-Postest, Control Simple Randomized

18 Assume that the SMSG math program is more effective
than the usual math program. If, however, the teacher in the usual math program were more competent
than the SMSG teacher, the true effect of the SMSG
program would be _____(reduced/increased).

∎ reduced

19 If the competence of the two teachers was consider-
ably different, the usual math program might appear
_____(more/less) effective than the SMSG program.

∎ more

20 To minimize the effect of teacher differences on the
two treatment groups, it would be best to have _____
(many/few) teachers independently conducting treatment groups.

∎ many

21 When it is possible to have many teachers in a study, in addition to assigning students randomly to treatments, it is desirable to also _____ assign teachers to treatments.

■ randomly

22 To reduce the effect of teacher differences on the dependent variable, the study can be structured to minimize these differences. The Random Replications Model, given as Model 17-2, reduces the effect of such differences by providing a number of repetitions for each treatment. Each repetition is technically called a _____ .

■ replication

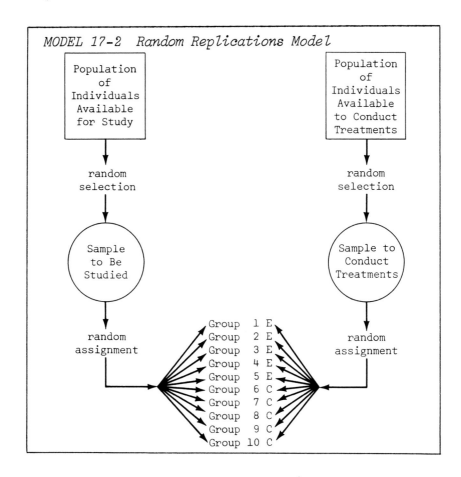

MODEL 17-2 Random Replications Model

Population of Individuals Available for Study

Population of Individuals Available to Conduct Treatments

random selection

random selection

Sample to Be Studied

Sample to Conduct Treatments

random assignment

random assignment

Group 1 E
Group 2 E
Group 3 E
Group 4 E
Group 5 E
Group 6 C
Group 7 C
Group 8 C
Group 9 C
Group 10 C

23 Note that in this model there are _____ popula-
tion(s).

■
■ two

24 After randomly selecting a sample from the population of individuals available for study, this sample
is randomly assigned to _____ experimental and
_____ control groups.

■
■ five, five

25 The next step is to select individuals from the population of those available to conduct treatments. It
will be necessary to select _____ such individuals.

■
■ ten

26 After ten such individuals have been randomly selected to conduct the treatments, they are then
_____ assigned to the ten groups.

■
■ randomly

27 In effect, the Random Replications Model serves two
purposes: first, it controls for the differential
effects of _____ variables; second, it random-
izes any individual differences among those conducting the _____ .

■
■ extraneous, treatments

28 The model used in this study requires _____ selec-
    tion and _____ assignment of both students and
    teachers.

■
■ random, random

29 Although there are five experimental and five con-
    trol groups, the study is not concerned with any par-
    ticular replication. Rather, the overall effective-
    ness of the _____ method and the _____ method
    are to be compared.

■
■ ITA, Look-Say

30 The number of children in a class may relate to their ability to learn to read. By having the same number of children in each class, you have control-led for the effects of this _____ independent variable.

■ extraneous

31 Therefore, the size of class _____ (is/is not) likely to affect the results of this study.

■ is not

32 Variables relating to student and teacher character-istics are assumed to be _____ distributed among the two groups.

■ randomly

33 Randomly assigning teachers to the treatment groups assumes they are equally able to teach the _____ and the _____ methods of reading.

■ ITA, Look-Say

34 The likelihood of any particular teacher having an effect on the results of a study using the Random Replications Model is _____ (less/greater) than for the Simple Randomized Model.

■ less

18.

SIMPLE FACTORIAL MODELS

1 The Simple Randomized Model controls for the effects of extraneous variables by the process of
_____ .

■ randomization

2 In the Simple Randomized Model, we sampled individuals _____(with/without) stratifying the sample on some nonmanipulated independent variable.

■ without

3 Therefore, the Simple Randomized Model _____ (does/does not) enable us to determine the differential effect of the treatments at varying levels of some nonmanipulated variable.

■ does not

4   To determine the differential effect of treatments
    at different levels of a nonmanipulated variable,
    we must control for this variable by _____
    (randomization/homogeneity).

■   homogeneity

5   Controlling a nonmanipulated variable by homogeneity
    permits us to determine the effects of the manipu-
    lated variable on the dependent variable at differ-
    ent _____ of the nonmanipulated variable.

■   levels

6   The research structure that permits this is termed a
    Simple Factorial Model. This model controls for a
    nonmanipulated variable by _____(random-
    ization/homogeneity) rather than by _____
    (randomization/homogeneity).

■   homogeneity, randomization

MODEL 18-1   Simple Factorial Model (2x2)

Non-Manipulated Variable	Manipulated Variable	
	Treatment A	Treatment B
Level I	Cell 1	Cell 3
Level II	Cell 2	Cell 4

7 Model 18-1 is a graphic representation of a 2x2
   Simple Factorial Model. In this model the nonmanipulated variable to be controlled by homogeneity is
   termed the _____ variable.

■ control

8 There are _____ treatments of the manipulated variable and _____ levels of the nonmanipulated variable.

■ two, two

9 Therefore, there are _____ cells into which the sample is divided.

■ four

10 The individuals in cell 1 are receiving treatment ___
   of the manipulated variable and are at level ___ of
   the nonmanipulated variable.

■ A, I

11 The individuals receiving treatment B who are at
   Level I of the nonmanipulated variable are in cell __.

■ 3

12 This is called a treatment-by-level model because
   there are _____ of the manipulated variable
   and _____ of the nonmanipulated variable.

■ treatments, levels

13 This simple factorial model includes two treatments
    of cognitive training and two levels of _____.

■ intelligence

14 Intelligence is the _____(manipulated/
    nonmanipulated) variable.

■ nonmanipulated

15 The dependent variable is the students' _____ ability.

■ transfer

16 The scores in the four cells represent the mean (average) scores for the _____ variable.

■ dependent

17 The mean transfer score for the treatment A, low IQ group is _____ .

■ 16.5

18 The mean scores for the four cells represent the combinations of _____ by _____ .

■ treatments, levels

19 In addition to the four cell scores, there are four marginal mean scores: _____ for rows and _____ for columns.

■ two, two

20 The marginal column means are for the two _____ and the marginal row means are for the two _____ .

■ treatments, levels

21 The mean transfer scores for treatments A and B are
    _____ and _____ respectively.

■
■ 26.2, 27.2

22 The treatment mean scores are termed the main effect
    for treatments. The difference between the means of
    the treatment main effects is _____ point(s).

■
■ one

23 The main effect for treatments _____(does/does
    not) take into account any differential effect that
    results from level of IQ.

■
■ does not

24 The mean of transfer scores for the low IQ level is
    _____ and for the high IQ level is _____ .

■
■ 20.2, 33.1

25 The level mean scores, without regard to treatments,
    are termed the main effect for _____ .

■
■ levels

26 The main effect for levels _____(does/does not)
    take into account any differential effect from treat-
    ments.

■
■ does not

27 The difference between the means of the main effect for levels is _____ point(s).

■ 12.9

28 The differences between the main effect for levels is _____(smaller/larger) than the main effect for treatments.

■ larger

29 Thus far the simple factorial model has enabled us to arrive at two independent estimates of the effectiveness of the study: one for the main effect of _____ and one for the main effect of _____ .

■ treatments, levels

30 The difference between the means for levels of intelligence is _____(less/greater) for treatment B than for treatment A.

■ less

31 The influence of IQ on transfer ability is greater for treatment ___(A/B).

■ A

32 It _____(can/cannot) be concluded that treatment B is more effective than treatment A regardless of IQ level.

■ cannot

33 Treatment ___ appears to be more effective for the
    low IQ group and treatment ___ appears to be more ef-
    fective for the high IQ group.

■ B, A

34 Thus, a particular combination of treatment and le-
    vel of IQ interact to produce greater gains than
    some other combination. An advantage of the Simple
    Factorial Model is that you can examine the
    _____ between treatments and levels.

■ interaction

35 A graphic representation of the data in Study 18-1
    is shown below.

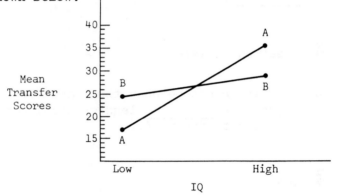

This graph illustrates the interaction effects between treatments and levels on the dependent variable of _____ ability.

■ transfer

36 Another way of stating that there is an interaction between treatment and levels is that the treatment and levels _____ (are/are not) independent of each other.

■ are not

37 In this study, then, it can be said that the effectiveness of a particular treatment is _____ _____ (dependent upon/independent of) IQ level.

■ dependent upon

38 This 2x2 Simple Factorial Model enabled us within one study to determine the main effects of two _____ , the main effects of two _____ of some control variable, and the interaction effects of the _____ and _____ .

■ treatments, levels, treatments, levels

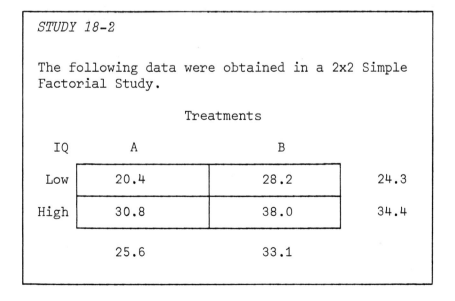

STUDY 18-2

The following data were obtained in a 2x2 Simple Factorial Study.

Treatments

IQ	A	B	
Low	20.4	28.2	24.3
High	30.8	38.0	34.4
	25.6	33.1	

39 In Study 18-2, the difference between the means for
    the treatment main effects is _____ points.

■ 7.5

40 The difference between the means for the level main
    effects is _____ points.

■ 10.1

41 Treatment ___ appears to be more effective than
    treatment___ .

■ B, A

42 Regardless of treatment, the _____(low/high) IQ
    group performs better than the _____(low/high) IQ
    group.

■ high, low

43 A graphic representation of the data in Study 18-2
is shown below.

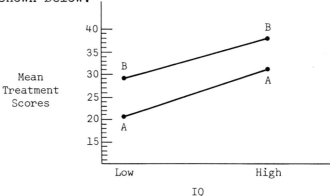

In this graph there appears to be _____(no/some)
differential effect of the treatments based on IQ
level.

■
■   no

44 Treatments and levels in this study _____(are/
are not) relatively independent of each other.

■
■   are

45 It can be concluded that there _____(is/is not)
an interaction effect between treatment and levels.

■
■   is not

46 The previous examples of simple factorial models il-
lustrated studies with one manipulated variable and
one _____ variable.

■
■   nonmanipulated

47 The 2x2 design need not be restricted in this manner but may include two _____ independent variables or two _____ independent variables.

∎ manipulated, nonmanipulated

STUDY 18-3

A college instructor compared the effects of class size as well as the introduction of programmed instruction on the learning of research methodology. He conducted a study using a 2x2 Simple Factorial Model.

Manipulated
Variable 2:
  Type of   Manipulated Variable 1:
Instruction   Class Size

	Small	Usual
Programmed		
Usual		

---

48 Study 18-3 is an _____ (experimental/nonexperimental) hypothesis-testing study.

∎ experimental

49 In this study _____ (one/both) variables have been manipulated.

∎ both

50 This study illustrates a 2x2 Simple Factorial Model
with _____(no/one/two) nonmanipulated variable(s).

■ no

51 There is(are) _____(no/one/two) manipulated varia-
ble(s).

■ two

52 Manipulated variable 1 is _____ _____ and manipulated variable 2 is _____ _____ _____ .

■ class size, type of instruction

53 The treatments of class size and type of instruction
both contain a "usual" group indicating that there
are two _____(experimental/control) groups
included in the study for comparative purposes.

■ control

54 In this study, there is(are) _____ manipulated vari-
able(s), _____ nonmanipulated variable(s), _____exper-
imental group(s), and _____ control group(s).

■ two, no, two, two

55 The treatment main effects for columns deal with the
variable of _____ _____ .

■ class size

56 The treatment main effects for rows deal with the variable of _____ ____ _____ .

■ type of instruction

57 This study design permits not only the independent analysis of the main effects for both independent variables but also an analysis of the _____ between the treatments.

■ interaction

58 If an instructor designed a 2x2 Simple Factorial Model comparing males and females and the students' chosen majors in college as they relate to knowledge of research methodology, both of these variables would be _____ (manipulated/nonmanipulated) variables.

■ nonmanipulated

MODEL 18-2 *Simple Factorial Model (4x3)*

Manipulated Variable

Nonmanipulated Variable	Treatment A	Treatment B	Treatment C	Treatment D
Level I	Cell 1	Cell 4	Cell 7	Cell 10
Level II	Cell 2	Cell 5	Cell 8	Cell 11
Level III	Cell 3	Cell 6	Cell 9	Cell 12

59 Model 18-2 is a Simple Factorial Model including
    four _____ of the manipulated variable and
    three _____ of the nonmanipulated variable.

■ treatments, levels

60 Whereas Model 18-1 is a 2x2 Simple Factorial Model,
    Model 18-2 is a ___ x ___ Simple Factorial Model.

■ 4x3

61 The Simple Factorial Model, then, need not be re-
    stricted to a 2x2 layout but can be generalized to
    any number of _____ and any number of
    _____ .

■ treatments, levels

62 In Model 18-2, there are ____ cells into which the
    sample is divided.

■ 12

63 The individuals in cell 1 are receiving treatment
    ____ and are at level ___ .

■ A, I

64 The individuals receiving treatment C and at level
    II are in cell ___ .

■ 8

65 A comparison of the means for the columns provides
    us with an estimate of the main effects for the
    _____ (treatments/levels).

■ treatments

66 A comparison of the means for the rows provides us
    with an estimate of the main effects for the
    _____ (treatments/levels).

■ levels

67 The column main effects are for the _____
    variable and the row main effects are for the
    _____ variable.

■ manipulated, nonmanipulated

68 In addition to the row and column main effects, the
    simple factorial model enables us to determine the
    _____ between treatments and levels.

■ interaction

19.

COMPLEX FACTORIAL MODELS

1 The Simple Factorial Model enables us to evaluate the main effects of two independent variables as well as the _____ between the two variables.

▪ interaction

2 To have interaction, there must be at least _____ independent variables in the study.

▪ two

3 The treatment by levels interaction in the Simple Factorial Model is termed a "first order interaction" because _____(only two/more than two) independent variables are involved.

▪ only two

4 If we wish to determine interaction beyond first
   order interactions, we must include in the design at
   least _____ independent variables.

■ three

5 Three independent variables within the same model
   will permit us to determine _____ (first/second)
   order interactions.

■ second

6 The Complex Factorial Model permits us to determine
   the interaction between three or more independent
   variables, thus enabling us to obtain at least
   _____ order interactions.

■ second

7 Of course, factorial models, in addition to determining interaction, enable us to determine the main effects of the independent variables. In the Simple
   Factorial Model, we have only two main effects. In
   the Complex Factorial Model, we would have at least
   _____ main effects.

■ three

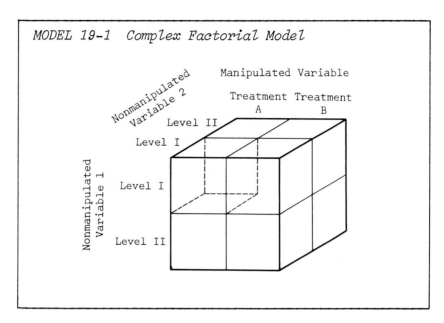

MODEL 19-1 Complex Factorial Model

8 Model 19-1 is a Complex Factorial Model including
   _____ variable(s), and _____ nonmanipulated varia-
   ble(s).

■ one, two

9 In this Complex Factorial Model, the manipulated variable includes _____ treatments and each of the nonmanipulated variables include _____ levels.

■ two, two

10 This design is a 2x2x2 Complex Factorial Model,
    thereby containing a total of _____ cells.

■ eight

11 The outlined cell is for treatment ___ , level ___ of nonmanipulated variable 1, and level ___ of non-manipulated variable 2.

■ A, I, I

12 It is possible to determine the main effects for _____ independent variables.

■ three

13 The three main effects are for the _____ var-iable and for each of the _____ variables.

■ manipulated, nonmanipulated

14 With three independent variables, the first order interactions are for each possible pair of variables. In this case, three such interactions are possible:

manipulated variable with _____ ,
manipulated variable with _____ ,
nonmanipulated variable 1 with _____ .

■ nonmanipulated variable 1, nonmanipulated variable 2, nonmanipulated variable 2

15 Second order interactions require the inclusion of _____ independent variables, the minimum for a Com-plex Factorial Model.

■ three

16 This model permits the analysis of _____ (one/more than one) second order interaction(s).

■ one

17 Main effects and interactions for Model 19-1 are:

Main Effects:

Manipulated Variable (MV)
Nonmanipulated Variable 1 (NMV1)
Nonmanipulated Variable 2 (NMV2)

First Order Interactions:

MVxNMV1
MVxNMV2
NMV1xNMV2

Second Order Interaction:

MVxNMV1xNMV2

As shown above, main effects deal with the effects of each independent variable taken _____ (singly/ in pairs).

■ singly

18 The analysis of the main effects of MV is conducted independent of the effects of _____ and _____ .

■ NMV1, NMV2

19 The analysis of the main effects of NMV1 is conducted independent of the effects of _____ and ____ .

■ NMV2, MV

20 The analysis of the main effects of NMV2 is conducted independent of the effects of ____ and _____ .

∎ MV, NMV1

21 First order interactions deal with the effects of independent variables taken _____(singly/in pairs).

∎ in pairs

22 The analysis of the MVxNMV1 first order interaction is conducted independent of the effects of _____ .

∎ NMV2

23 The analysis of the MVxNMV2 first order interaction is conducted independent of the effects of _____ .

∎ NMV1

24 The analysis of the NMV1xNMV2 first order interaction is conducted independent of the effects of ____ .

∎ MV

25 Second order interactions deal with effects of independent variables taken in _____(pairs/triplets).

∎ triplets

26 The simultaneous effect of MVxNMV1xNMV2 provides an
    estimate of the _____ order interaction of these
    variables.

■
■ second

27 Here is a table of the data layout for Model 19-1.

                    Manipulated Variable

		Treatment A		Treatment B	
Nonmanipulated Variable 1 Level		Nonmanipulated Variable 2 Level I	Nonmanipulated Variable 2 Level II	Nonmanipulated Variable 2 Level I	Nonmanipulated Variable 2 Level II
	I	Cell 1	Cell 3	Cell 5	Cell 7
	II	Cell 2	Cell 4	Cell 6	Cell 8

    The above table presents a two-dimensional layout
    of Model 19-1. Cell 1 corresponds to cell ___ in
    Model 19-1.

■
■ 1

28 There are _____ cells within treatment A and _____
    cells within treatment B.

■
■ four, four

29 The analysis of the data for treatments A and B pro-
    vides a test of the main effects for the _____
    variable.

■
■ manipulated

30 To determine the main effect for the manipulated var-
    iable, it is necessary to compare the combined data
    in cells ___ , ___ , ___ , and ___ for treatment A,
    with the combined data in cells ___ , ___ , ___ ,
    and ___ for treatment B.

■
■   1,2,3,4 5,6,7,8

31 By combining the data within each treatment, we ob-
    tain the main effect for MV independent of _____
    and _____ .

■
■   NMV1, NMV2

32 Because there are two levels of NMV1, to determine
    the main effect for this variable it is necessary to
    compare the data for the cells included in
    _____ ___ with the data for the cells included in
    _____ ___ for this variable.

■
■   level I, level II

33 Thus, to determine the main effect for NMV1, it is
    necessary to compare the combined data in cells ___ ,
    ___ , ___ , and ___ with the combined data in cells
    ___ , ___ , ___ , and ___ .

■
■   1,3,5,7 2,4,6,8

34 By combining the data in the cells in this manner,
    we analyze the main effects of NMV1 independent of
    the effects of ___ and _____ .

■
■   MV, NMV2

35 Because there are two levels of NMV2, to determine
the main effect for this variable it is necessary to
compare the data for the cells included in _____
___ with the data for the cells included in _____
____ for this variable.

■ level I, level II

36 To determine the main effect for NMV2, it is necessary to compare the combined data in cells ___ ,
___ , ___ , and ___ with the combined data in cells
___ , ___ , ___ , and ___ .

■ 1,2,5,6 3,4,7,8

37 To obtain the first order interaction for MVxNMV1,
it is necessary to ignore _____ .

■ NMV2

38 By ignoring NMV2, the analysis deals with the interaction effects of _____ independent variables.

■ two

39 Because in ignoring NMV2 we are dealing only with a
first order interaction, this is a _____(simple/
complex) factorial analysis.

■ simple

40 To analyze the MVxNMV1 interaction, it is possible
to prepare the data as a 2x2 layout. Below is the
2x2 matrix for this purpose. Indicate within each
cell the combination of the original cells for this
analysis.

Manipulated Variable

Nonmanipulated
Variable 1   Treatment A   Treatment B

Level I | | |
|---|---|
Level II | | |

Cells 1,3	Cells 5,7
Cells 2,4	Cells 6,8

41 To obtain the first order interaction for MVxNMV2 it
is necessary to ignore _____ .

NMV1

42 To analyze the MVxNMV2 interaction, it is possible to convert the original cells to a 2x2 layout. Indicate within each cell the combinations of cells for this analysis.

	Manipulated Variable	
Nonmanipulated Variable 2	Treatment A	Treatment B
Level I		
Level II		

■
■

Cells 1,2	Cells 5,6
Cells 3,4	Cells 7,8

43 To obtain the first order interaction for NMV1xNMV2 it is necessary to ignore ____ .

■
■ MV

44 To analyze the NMV1xNMV2 interaction, it is possible
    to convert the original cells to a 2x2 layout. Indi-
    cate within each cell the combinations of cells for
    this analysis.

                                    Nonmanipulated Variable 2

Nonmanipulated Variable 1   Level I   Level II

                    Level I

                    Level II

Cells 1,5	Cells 3,7
Cells 2,6	Cells 4,8

45 Thus, the analysis of the three first order inter-
    actions are essentially _____(simple/complex)
    factorial analyses.

    simple

46 The analysis of the second order interaction
    _____(would/would not) ignore one of the inde-
    pendent variables.

    would not

47 Because MV, NMV1, and NMV2 are analyzed simultane-
    ously, we will obtain a _____ order interaction.

    second

48 A model that enables us to take into account three
    or more independent variables simultaneously is cal-
    led a _____ _____ Model.

■
■ Complex Factorial

49 The Complex Factorial Model need not be restricted
    to a 2x2x2 design but can be generalized to any num-
    ber and combination of _____ and
    _____ independent variables.

■
■ manipulated, nonmanipulated

50 Of course, the greater the number of independent vari-
    ables included in a complex factorial model, the
    higher the order of _____ analyses possible.

■
■ interaction

PART

VIII∎

THE USE OF STATISTICS IN RESEARCH

We have discussed the necessity of obtaining representative samples to permit inferences regarding population values. However, no matter how careful one
is in selecting a sample, it is not possible to
eliminate all error from the data.

Sets 20, 21, and 22 discuss how statistical procedures are employed in research, and how they permit
inference from sample values to population values.

Set 20 introduces the concept of "sampling error"
and discusses how statistical techniques permit the
researcher to determine the probability that obtained differences between samples result from random
errors in sampling rather than *real* differences in
the effect of the independent variable. The statistical hypothesis called the "null hypothesis" is
introduced and an explanation is given of its use in
the statistical treatment of research data.

In making a decision to reject or not reject the
null hypothesis, a researcher always takes some risk
of being incorrect. Set 21 provides an introduction
to the statistical evaluation of hypotheses and indicates how the researcher interprets probability levels in his decision regarding the null hypothesis.
Examples are given to illustrate the use of statistically determined probability levels in the interpretation of data. The probability levels generally
used as the criteria for rejection of the null

hypothesis are presented as well as the commonly used symbolic notations for indicating probability levels.

When a researcher has determined the probability level associated with the rejection of a null hypothesis, he decides whether to reject it. Although he knows the probability level, there are two types of errors he can make in rejecting or not rejecting the null hypothesis. Set 21 defines the Type I and Type II errors and illustrates their importance in interpreting statistical findings.

Set 22 discusses significance levels and how they are used in making decisions regarding the null hypothesis. The common factors that affect significance levels are presented, and examples illustrate how these factors influence the interpretation of statistical findings.

SET

20.

STATISTICAL CONCEPTS IN RESEARCH: SAMPLING ERROR

1   We know that it is usually impossible to measure the
    entire population. Most research hypotheses are ex-
    amined by selecting a _____ from a population.

■ sample

2   To make valid inferences regarding a population, it
    is necessary for the sample to be _____
    of the population.

■ representative

3   The most common method of obtaining a sample that is
    representative of a population is to select it
    _____ from the population.

■ randomly

4 When we employ proper sampling techniques, we can be relatively certain the sample is _____ of the population from which it is selected.

■ representative

5 Although a representative sample can be obtained by employing proper sampling techniques, it usually _____(is/is not) possible to select a sample that exactly represents a population.

■ is not

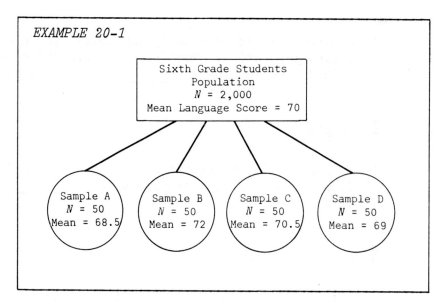

EXAMPLE 20-1

Sixth Grade Students
Population
N = 2,000
Mean Language Score = 70

Sample A
N = 50
Mean = 68.5

Sample B
N = 50
Mean = 72

Sample C
N = 50
Mean = 70.5

Sample D
N = 50
Mean = 69

6 In Example 20-1 the population of 2,000 sixth grade students has a mean language score of _____ .

■ 70

7   A researcher randomly selected four samples of 50
    students each from this population. The mean scores
    of the samples he selected were _____ , ____ ,
    _____ , and ____ .

■   68.5, 72, 70.5, 69

8   The mean language score of sample A is _____
    (smaller/larger) than the population mean language
    score.

■   smaller

9   The mean score of sample B is _____ (smaller/
    larger) than the population mean score.

■   larger

10 Although samples A and B have been randomly selected,
    the mean language scores of these samples differ
    from the mean language score of the _____ .

■   population

11 The mean language scores of the four samples _____
    from the population mean score.

■   differ

12 Even using proper sampling techniques, the researcher
    did not obtain a sample mean score in any of his sam-
    ples that was exactly equal to the _____ _____.

■   population mean

13 Because none of the four sample means exactly equal-
led the population mean, there is some error in the
mean scores of the _____ .

■ samples

14 The error in the mean scores of samples does not result from improper sampling techniques. It is the
chance error involved in selecting samples and is
referred to as sampling _____ .

■ error

15 Sampling error is always present when samples are
selected. It results not from improper sampling
techniques of the researcher but from _____ .

■ chance

16 The variability among the sample mean scores in the
four samples is the result of _____ _____ .

■ sampling error

17 Because of sampling error, the mean score of a sample is likely to vary from the mean score of the
_____ .

■ population

18 Thus, because of _____ _____ , we are never
   certain that a sample mean score reflects the population mean score exactly.

■ sampling error

19 Suppose the population mean of sixth grade students'
   arithmetic scores is 65. If we selected a sample
   using proper sampling techniques, it is likely that
   the sample mean score would _____ _____
   (equal exactly/only approximate) 65.

■ only approximate

20 Regardless of how carefully you select a sample, sample values usually only approximate population values. Thus, a sample mean score usually _____
   (will/will not) equal exactly the population mean
   score.

■ will not

21 Because it is difficult to obtain a sample that is
   exactly representative of a population, it is likely
   that the mean score of a sample will be _____
   _____(the same as/different from) the population
   mean score.

■ different from

```
STUDY 20-1

A junior high school physical education teacher
wished to test the hypothesis that the basket-
ball accuracy of eighth grade boys is greater
than the accuracy of eighth grade girls.  He ran-
domly selected a sample of boys and a sample of
girls and measured their accuracy.  The boys'
score was 20 and the girls' was 19.
```

22 In Study 20-1 the teacher probably _____(would/
    would not) be justified in generalizing that eighth
    grade boys score higher than eighth grade girls.

■
■ would not

23 The teacher would not be justified in concluding
    that eighth grade boys were better than eighth grade
    girls in basketball accuracy because the difference
    in the scores he obtained could result from

    _____ _____ .

■
■ sampling error

24 Statistical techniques are available to determine
    the probability of whether differences obtained be-
    tween samples represent true differences in the
    _____ or result from _____ error.

■
■ population, sampling

25 Because we usually do not know population values, we
    must make inferences regarding population values
    from _____ values.

■
■ sample

26 When we employ statistical techniques to determine the probability that an inference regarding a population value is correct, we are making a _____ inference.

■ statistical

27 The use of statistical techniques permits us to make inferences from sample values to population values by measuring the _____ that our inferences are correct.

■ probability

28 Research is generally concerned with determining probability levels associated with hypotheses. The statement "boys are more accurate at basketball than girls" is a _____ .

■ hypothesis

29 Data have been obtained for two samples drawn from the population of eighth graders. By statistical techniques we wish to determine the _____ level that our hypothesis is correct.

■ probability

30 Statistical techniques permit us to calculate the _____ that two samples come from the same population.

■ probability

31 In Study 20-1, the research hypothesis states that the boys' scores and the girls' scores come from _____ (different/the same) population(s) of basketball scores.

■ different

32 Thus, this research hypothesis is concerned with _____ population(s) of scores.

■ two

33 Statistical techniques are generally not used to directly test whether two samples come from different populations. Instead, we usually are interested in determining the probability that samples come from the _____ population.

■ same

34 The research hypothesis is stated in terms of more than one population. To make a statistical test, the statistician usually rewords the hypothesis in a form called the *null hypothesis*, so that it is concerned with the scores of _____ population.

■ one

35 The research hypothesis reworded as a null hypothesis is, "There is ____ difference in basketball accuracy scores of boys and girls."

■ no

36 The null hypothesis that there is no difference in the basketball accuracy scores between boys and girls is the same as saying both samples were selected from the same _____ .

■ population

37 To test the null hypothesis means that we are testing whether or not the boys and girls came from the same _____ insofar as basketball accuracy is concerned.

■ population

38 Statistical techniques which enable us to determine the probability of being incorrect if we reject the hypothesis that the samples come from the same population provide a test of the _____(research/ null) hypothesis.

■ null

39 If there is no difference between the mean basketball shooting scores of the samples of boys and girls, we can infer that there is ____ difference in the shooting scores of the _____ of boys and girls.

■ no, population

40 Therefore, we may infer that if the means of two samples do not differ, they both come from the same _____ .

■ population

41 However, we have learned that the mean scores of two
    samples of the same population are hardly ever ex-
    actly the same because of _____ error.

■ sampling

42 The sample mean score of the boys _____(does/
    does not) differ from the sample mean score of the
    girls.

■ does

43 The mean score of two samples may differ somewhat,
    because of sampling error, even if the samples have
    been selected from the same _____ .

■ population

44 Statistical techniques permit us to determine the
    probability that the difference between samples re-
    sults from _____ _____ .

■ sampling error

45 To test a research hypothesis, the researcher is not
    interested in making statements that are limited to
    _____(samples/populations).

■ samples

46 Statistical techniques permit the researcher to deter-
    mine the probability that the null hypothesis is in-
    correct—that the two samples come from _____
    (the same/different) population(s).

■ different

47 Thus, the researcher is concerned with determining
    the _____ that the _____ hypothesis is in-
    correct.

■ probability, null

48 When we test the null hypothesis we are asking the
    question, "What is the probability that the differ-
    ence obtained between sample means comes from sam-
    pling _____?"

■ error

49 In effect, we wish to determine the probability that
    the _____ hypothesis is incorrect.

■ null

50 In Study 20-1, the researcher wished to determine
    the probability that the obtained difference between
    the means of boys and girls resulted from _____
    _____ .

■ sampling error

SET

21∎

STATISTICAL EVALUATION OF HYPOTHESES

1 We have learned that mean scores of samples will
   vary even when they come from the same population.
   This results from _____ _____ .

∎ sampling error

2 Concluding that the difference between sample means
   comes from sampling error justifies the researcher
   in ___ _____(rejecting/not rejecting) the null
   hypothesis.

∎ not rejecting

3 Rejecting the null hypothesis means the researcher
   is concluding that the samples _____(do/do not)
   come from the same population.

∎ do not

4 If a researcher concludes that the samples come from the same population, he is attributing the difference between the sample means to _____ _____ .

■ sampling error

5 By using statistical techniques, the researcher can determine the probability that two samples come from the same _____ .

■ population

6 If the researcher can demonstrate that the difference between sample means has a high probability of resulting from sampling error, he is justified in concluding that the samples come from the same _____ .

■ population

7 Thus, the use of statistical techniques provide the researcher with the probability that he is wrong if he decides to reject the _____ hypothesis.

■ null

8 A researcher is justified in not rejecting the null hypothesis when a statistical test indicates there is a high probability that the difference between sample means results from _____ _____ .

■ sampling error

9　A researcher who determines, by a statistical test, that there is a 40 percent probability the null hypothesis is incorrect would be justified in _____ _____(rejecting/not rejecting) the null hypothesis.

■ not rejecting

10　The researcher will reject the null hypothesis only when there is a very _____(low/high) probability that this decision is incorrect.

■ low

11　To test the null hypothesis, then, the researcher must determine, by statistical techniques, the _____ that the difference between samples comes from _____ _____.

■ probability, sampling error

12　Although probability is generally thought of in percentage terms, in research it is usually reported in decimal form with the symbol P representing probability. Thus, the expression "$P = .25$" is read as "the probability is equal to ____ percent."

■ 25

13　Another way of interpreting the expression "$P = .25$" is "there are 25 chances in _____ ."

■ 100

14 If a researcher determines that the probability of
    being wrong in rejecting the null hypothesis is $P =$
    .35, this means that there is a probability of _____
    that the difference between the sample means resulted
    from _____ _____ .

■ .35, sampling error

15 If there is a probability of $P =$ .05 or less that
    sample differences result from sampling error, re-
    searchers generally will reject the null hypothesis.
    This is the same as saying "There is such a small
    probability that the sample differences resulted
    from sampling error that I will reject the hypothe-
    sis that the two samples came from the same
    _____ ."

■ population

16 The symbol < means "less than." The expression "$P <$
    .05" is read as "the probability is _____ _____
    .05."

■ less than

17 Conversely, the symbol > means "greater than." The
    expression "the probability is greater than .05"
    would be written as _____ .

■ $P >$ .05

18 Researchers in the behavioral sciences generally reject the null hypothesis if the probability is
_____ $(P < .05/P > .05)$ that sample differences
come from sampling error.

■ $P < .05$

19 If the probability that the null hypothesis is correct is $P < .05$, researchers will generally _____
(reject/not reject) the null hypothesis.

■ reject

20 If a statistical test indicates the probability is
$P > .05$ that two samples came from the same population, researchers generally ____ _____ (reject/not
reject) the null hypothesis.

■ not reject

STUDY 21-1

A researcher studying the difference in reading
ability of two samples of students obtained the
following data:

        Sample A: Mean Reading Score = 72
        Sample B: Mean Reading Score = 69

He performed a statistical test and determined
that the probability of being incorrect in rejecting the null hypothesis is $P = .16$.

---

21 In Study 21-1, the researcher obtained a mean difference between Sample A and Sample B of _____ points.

■ three

22 Stating the null hypothesis is the same as saying
that Sample A and Sample B came from _____(one/two)
population(s).

■ one

23 Assume the researcher designates $P = .05$ as the highest probability level at which he is willing to reject the null hypothesis. In this study the researcher obtained a probability level of $P =$ _____ .
Therefore, he should ___ _____(reject/not reject)
the null hypothesis.

■ .16, not reject

24 The researcher should not reject the null hypothesis
because he obtained a probability level which was
_____(smaller/larger th

■ larger

25 The obtained probability level was _____$(P < .05/$
$P > .05)$.

■ $P > .05$

26 The probability was $P > .05$ that the difference between the mean scores of the two samples came from
_____ _____ .

■ sampling error

27 The obtained probability level of $P = .16$ was too
large a probability to permit the researcher to
_____(reject/not reject) the null hypothesis.

■ reject

STUDY 21-2

A college instructor wished to determine if there
was a difference between freshmen and sophomores
on an English composition test. The instructor
selected $P = .05$ as the level for rejecting the
null hypothesis. He randomly selected a freshman
class and a sophomore class and tested them. He
obtained the following data:

      Freshman Class: Mean Score = 50
     Sophomore Class: Mean Score = 38

Statistical analysis of these data yielded a
probability level of $P = .02$.

---

28 In Study 21-2, the freshman and sophomore samples
show a mean difference of ____ points.

■ 12

29 The null hypothesis being tested is "There is no
    _____ between freshmen and sophomores in
    English composition."

■ difference

30 This null hypothesis means that the obtained 12
    point difference between the two classes came from

    _____ _____ .

■ sampling error

31 The instructor obtained a probability of $P = $ _____ .
    This obtained probability is _____ $(P < .05/$
    $P > .05)$.

■ .02, $P < .05$

32 Because the obtained probability of $P = .02$ is less
    than $P = .05$, the instructor should _____
    (reject/not reject) the null hypothesis.

■ reject

33 By rejecting the null hypothesis, the instructor is
    asserting that the difference he obtained between
    the two mean scores reflects a true difference in
    the _____ .

■ population

34 The instructor should reject the null hypothesis because his statistical test has shown there is a very
small probability his obtained difference came from

_____ _____ .

■ sampling error

35 Although researchers in the behavioral sciences generally require P = .05 as the probability level at
which they reject the null hypothesis, some require
P = .01, which is a _____(more/less) stringent level than P = .05.

■ more

36 The phrase P = .05 is read as "There is a ___ percent
probability that the sample mean difference resulted
from sampling error." The phrase P = .01 is read as
"There is a ___ percent probability that the sample
mean difference resulted from sampling error."

■ 5, 1

37 If we decide to reject the null hypothesis at P =
.01 we are _____(more/less) confident we have made
the correct decision than if we had chosen P = .05.

■ more

38 There is less probability that we have made an incorrect decision in rejecting the null hypothesis if we
choose _____(P = .01/P = .05) as the acceptable
level for rejection.

■ P = .01

39 If the instructor had chosen $P = .01$ as his probability level for rejecting the null hypothesis, he would have ____ _____ (rejected/not rejected) the null hypothesis.

∎ not rejected

40 Using $P = .01$ the instructor would not have rejected the null hypothesis because his obtained probability was _____ (less/greater) than $P = .01$.

∎ greater

41 The decision to reject the null hypothesis depends upon the _____ level we choose for rejection.

∎ probability

42 If we choose $P = .05$ we have chosen a _____ (more/less) stringent probability level for rejection than if we choose $P = .01$.

∎ less

43 The purpose of certain statistical tests is to provide the researcher with the probability that his obtained differences between samples come from _____ _____ .

∎ sampling error

44 Based on a statistical test, the researcher makes a decision whether to _____ or _____ the null hypothesis.

■ reject, not reject

45 Before a researcher begins his study, he should designate the _____ level at which he is willing to risk being wrong if he decides to reject the null hypothesis.

■ probability

46 If the researcher decides to reject the null hypothesis at $P = .05$, this is called his designated level for significance. If, by a statistical test, he obtains a probability level of $P = .17$, this would be considered _____ (significant/nonsignificant).

■ nonsignificant

47 If he had obtained a probability level of $P = .03$, this would be considered _____ (significant/nonsignificant).

■ significant

48 When a researcher makes the statement "There was a significant difference between the sample means," this is the same as saying he has _____ the null hypothesis.

■ rejected

49 When he says that the difference between the sample
   means was nonsignificant, he _____ rejected the
   null hypothesis.

■ has not

50 A null hypothesis that is rejected at $P = .05$ means
   that there is ___ percent probability that the obtained difference between the sample means come from
   sampling error.

■ 5

51 Thus, even if we decide to reject the null hypothesis at $P = .05$, there is a low _____ that we
   have made an error in rejecting it.

■ probability

52 When using sample data we are never able to reject
   the null hypothesis with absolute certainty: there
   is always some possibility that we are wrong, because of _____ error.

■ sampling

53 There are two types of errors we can make when deciding whether to reject the null hypothesis.

Type I error: Rejecting the null hypothesis on the basis of sample data, when, in fact, the samples came from the same population.

Type II error: Not rejecting the null hypothesis on the basis of sample data, when, in fact the samples came from different populations.

As indicated above, these two types of error are termed _____ error and _____ error.

Type I, Type II

54 If, on the basis of a statistical test, we have not rejected the null hypothesis when in fact the two samples were selected from different populations, we have made a Type ____(I/II) error.

II

55 If, on the basis of a statistical test, we have rejected the null hypothesis when in fact the samples were selected from the same population, we have made a Type ____(I/II) error.

I

56 In rejecting a null hypothesis, based on a statistical test of sample data, there is always some probability that we have made a Type I error, because the difference obtained may result from _____ error.

sampling

57 If we designate $P = .05$ as the level at which we will reject the null hypothesis, the probability that we will make a Type I error is only $P =$ _____ .

■
■ .05

58 If we designate $P = .01$ as the level at which we will reject the null hypothesis, the probability that we will make a Type I error is only $P =$ _____ .

■
■ .01

59 The lower the level we designate for rejecting the null hypothesis, the _____(smaller/greater) the probability of making a Type I error.

■
■ smaller

60 On the other hand, the lower the level we designate for rejecting the null hypothesis, the _____ (smaller/greater) the probability of making a Type II error.

■
■ greater

SET

22∎

FACTORS AFFECTING SIGNIFICANCE LEVELS

1 We can determine the probability that the difference between two sample means results from sampling error by applying _____ techniques.

∎ statistical

2 Statistical techniques permit us to ascertain that the difference between sample means differ, because of sampling error, at a specific _____ level.

∎ probability

3 The probability level we obtain using statistical techniques is called the significance level. It is the probability that the difference between sample means comes from _____ _____ .

∎ sampling error

4 To say that the difference between two sample means
   is "significant at the .03 level" is the same as saying "The probability level that the difference between the sample means results from sampling error
   is $P =$ _____ ."

■
■ .03

5 Low probability levels are more significant than
   high levels. An obtained probability level of $P =$
   .07 is _____ (more/less) significant than an obtained probability level of $P =$ .11.

■
■ more

6 Other factors being equal, large differences between
   sample means are more _____ than small differences.

■
■ significant

7 This is because large differences between sample
   means are less likely to result from _____
   _____ than are small differences.

■
■ sampling error

8 The degree to which a difference between sample
   means is significant depends upon a number of factors. For example, other factors being equal, two
   sample means that differ by ten points will be _____
   (more/less) significant than two sample means that
   differ by five points.

■
■ more

9 One factor that affects the significance of the difference between sample means, then, is the magnitude of the _____ between the means.

■ difference

10 It stands to reason that, if we have used proper sampling techniques, large samples are _____(more/less) representative of a population than small samples.

■ more

11 The larger the samples, the less the probability that any difference between their means results from _____ _____ .

■ sampling error

12 Other factors being equal, the difference between mean scores of large samples is _____(more/less) significant than for small samples.

■ more

13 Thus, in addition to the magnitude of the difference between the means, the second factor affecting the significance level is the _____ of the samples.

■ size

```
STUDY 22-1

A researcher has obtained the following sets of
data:

A-B Comparison

    Sample A          N = 50          Mean Score = 20
    Sample B          N = 50          Mean Score = 30

C-D Comparison

    Sample C          N = 10          Mean Score = 20
    Sample D          N = 10          Mean Score = 30
```

14 In Study 22-1, the difference between the means of
    samples A and B is _____(the same as/
    different from) the difference between the means of
    samples C and D.

■ the same as

15 The number of individuals (N) in each sample in the
    A-B comparison is ____ . The N of each sample in
    the C-D comparison is ____ .

■ 50, 10

16 Other factors being equal, the difference between
    the means is more likely to come from sampling error
    in the ____(A-B/C-D) comparison.

■ C-D

17 This is because the size of the samples is smaller in the _____(A-B/C-D) comparison.

■ C-D

18 Other factors being equal, a statistical test of the difference between the means of samples A and B will yield a _____(higher/lower) significance level than the difference between samples C and D.

■ higher

19 Thus, other factors being equal, differences of the same magnitude are more _____ between large samples than between small samples.

■ significant

20 If there is a high degree of variability among the scores within each sample, it is reasonable to assume that the difference in means that comes from sampling error will be _____(smaller/larger) than if the scores within each sample have little variability.

■ larger

21 Homogeneity of the scores in each sample is likely to yield a _____(larger/smaller) difference because of sampling error between sample means.

■ smaller

22 Smaller differences between sample means are likely to occur because of sampling error if the scores within each sample are _____(homogeneous/heterogeneous).

■ homogeneous

STUDY 22-2

A researcher has obtained the following sets of data:

A-B Comparison

    Sample A N = 50   Mean Score = 20   SD = 5
    Sample B N = 50   Mean Score = 30   SD = 5

C-D Comparison

    Sample C N = 50   Mean Score = 20   SD = 7
    Sample D N = 50   Mean Score = 30   SD = 7

---

23 In Study 22-2, the difference between the means of samples A and B is _____(the same as/different from) the difference between the means of samples C and D.

■ the same as

24 The number of individuals (N) in each sample of the A-B comparison is _____(the same as/different from) the N in each sample of the C-D comparison.

■ the same as

25 The abbreviation SD stands for standard deviation, a measure of the variability of the scores within a sample. There is more variability within the samples in the _____(A-B/C-D) comparison.

■ C-D

26 Other factors being equal, the difference between the means is more likely to come from sampling error in the _____(A-B/C-D) comparison.

■ C-D

27 This is because there is more _____ within the samples in the C-D comparison.

■ variability

28 Other factors being equal, a statistical test of the difference between samples A and B will yield a _____(higher/lower) significance level than the difference between samples C and D.

■ higher

29 Other factors being equal, the same magnitude of difference between the means of homogeneous samples will be _____(less/more) significant than it will for heterogeneous samples.

■ more

30 Other factors being equal, the less variability among scores within the samples, the _____ (less/more) significant will be the difference between their mean scores.

■ more

31 Therefore, the third factor affecting the significance level is the _____ of the scores within each sample.

■ variability

32 We have identified three factors that affect the significance level:

1. The _____ of the difference between sample means.
2. The _____ of the samples.
3. The _____ of the scores within the samples.

■ magnitude, size, variability

33 A fourth factor that affects the significance level is the type of research hypothesis we have made. Recall that there are two types of research hypotheses: directional and _____ .

■ nondirectional

34 A directional hypothesis is one that predicts the _____ of the difference between mean scores.

■ direction

35 When the research hypothesis is nondirectional, we
will reject the null hypothesis if the obtained difference between sample means is sufficiently large,
regardless of the _____ of the differences.

■ direction

36 With a directional hypothesis, we will reject it
only if the difference is in the hypothesized
_____ .

■ direction

37 When we make a directional hypothesis, we are concerned with determining if sample means differ significantly only in the predicted direction. We
evaluate the significance of the difference between
sample means regardless of the direction when we
make a _____ hypothesis.

■ nondirectional

38 When the researcher is justified in stating the
hypothesis in directional terms, the statistical
test will yield lower P values than if the hypothesis were stated in nondirectional terms. (The reason for this belongs to the study of statistics and
is beyond the scope of this book.) Thus, it is to
the researcher's advantage to make a _____
(directional/nondirectional) hypothesis if there is
some basis for so doing.

■ directional

39 If the null hypothesis is based on a nondirectional research hypothesis, a given difference between sample means will be _____(more/less) significant than if it is based on a directional hypothesis.

■ less

40 An obtained difference between sample means will be _____(more/less) significant if the research hypothesis is directional rather than nondirectional.

■ more

41 Thus, a fourth factor affecting the significance level is whether the research hypothesis is _____ or _____ .

■ directional, nondirectional

42 The four factors that affect the significance level are:

1. The _____ of the difference between sample means.
2. The _____ of the samples.
3. The _____ of the scores within the samples.
4. Whether the research hypothesis is _____ or _____ .

■ magnitude, size, variability, directional, nondirectional

Index